THE SPIRIT AND SPLENDOUR OF
ART DECO

THE SPIRIT

ART

ALAIN LESIEUTRE

AND SPLENDOUR OF

DECO

CASTLE BOOKS

Library of Congress Cataloging in Publication Data

Lesieutre, Alain, 1931—
   The spirit and splendour of art deco.

   1. Art deco—History. I. Title.
N6494.A7L47 709'.04 73-20958
ISBN 0-8467-0029-8

ISBN 0–8467–0029–8
Library of Congress Catalog Card Number 73–20958
Copyright 1974 Paddington Press Ltd
Printed in the U.S.A.

Designed by Richard Browner

Research by Lynne Thornton

Arrangement has been made to publish this edition by Castle Books,
a division of Book Sales Inc. of Secaucus, New Jersey

September—1978

CONTENTS

7   INTRODUCTION

51   PAINTING

87   SCULPTURE

131 FURNITURE

163 FASHION

197 CERAMICS

219 GLASS

247 LACQUER

267 METALWORK

289 JEWELLERY

303 BIBLIOGRAPHY

INTRODUCTION

This is not a book for people who are embarassed by splendour or put off by luxury. The phenomenon documented here is the last attempt made in Europe to create a full-blooded, perfectly coherent decorative style, with its own completeness, its own internal logic, and its own dream.

In the context, the word "dream" is important. Stylistic changes come about, not only because society alters, but because peoples' day-dreams change. Style is the most conspicuous of the mechanisms through which we hope to alter ourselves, to become what we should like to be. We think that, by creating a certain kind of environment, by wearing different clothes, we ourselves will become different, and closer to the ideal we have formulated. And to some extent at least the transformation, each time we undertake it, is always effective. Historians of the subject have noted how women's bodies seem to be transformed, in response to the demands of fashion; and we only have to visit a good production of a Restoration comedy to be reminded, by the mannerisms that the actors adopt, that our stance, our gestures, the very tone of voice we use, are all of them influenced by the concept of style.

But while we are always willing to impose a new style upon ourselves, at the same time we cannot resist undermining it, contradicting what it says. The ideal has to cede at some points to the notion of convenience; it has to make room for habits and customs which may have nothing to do with the dream itself. Style evolves through the pressure of events, of unexpected associations of ideas, but also through sheer indulgence, until the moment is reached when a particular line of development can be carried no further. And we must also remember that we do not like too many people to share our dreams—a style is always a matter of "us" against "them," a badge of exclusivity. The moment at which it becomes truly popular is the moment when it begins to decline.

I. *These chairs by Carlo Bugatti, dating from c. 1902, are more avant-garde than anything produced by Italian designers before the late 1960's.*

8

At its height Art Deco pursued exclusivity with single-minded passion. Everyone who comes to Deco objects for the first time is struck by the luxury of the materials of which they are made. This is particularly true of the furniture—macassar ebony, the preferred material of so many of the best cabinet-makers of the twenties, is a wood which, through both color and texture, insistently calls attention to itself. The shagreen and ivory used as trim by the same craftsmen have similar qualities. Art Deco glass, in total contrast to the fancifulness of Art Nouveau design in this field, has a massive opulence—the simple forms characteristic of Marinot are simple because the material itself is so magnificent, with its clouds of bubbles and flecks of metal leaf. Other craftsmen, such as Decorchement, made glass which rivals the precious hardstones rich men have always coveted.

11. *Art Nouveau designers were interested in built-in furniture, even though their efforts were rather clumsy. Here is a smoking room by Pierre Selmersheim shown in the Salon des Artistes Décorateurs, 1911 (Art et Décoration, 1911/1).*

One striking thing about Deco design is its avoidance of the pretty. Art Deco is smart, rather than pretty, and it has the toughness which this implies. This is one reason why the style was able to absorb so much from African design. It was not merely that the Cubists had taught people to look at African art with new eyes, but that the Deco designers and their clients were sophisticated enough to realize that it is the contrast between barbarism and luxury which raises luxury itself to the highest power. Looking at the pictures of Suzanne Talbot's apartment (PLATES X and XI), we recognize the shock value of the African stools which the designer, Eileen Gray, has placed in this ultra-refined setting.

Another interesting and significant aspect of Art Deco is its relationship to the Modern Movement. The objects associated with the style show

III. *L'Atelier Français. Empire influence here combines with hints taken from the Ballets Russes.*

IV. (OPPOSITE) *The sumptuous bedroom, with its oriental air, was designed by Paul Poiret's decorating firm, Martine (Art et Décoration 1924/2).*

many borrowings from modernist painting and sculpture. But we soon become conscious of the fact that there was a scarcely veiled hostility between the spirit of Deco and that of Modernism. Deco sustained the values of the past, while Modernism was committed to the future. What the Art Deco designers took over were certain motifs—Cubist ones chiefly—which they used for their own purposes. But these thefts should not deceive us into thinking there was an identity of aim.

But the confusion about the relationship between Art Deco and the Modern Movement is just one of a number of confusions and errors which have clouded our perceptions as the style began to be revived and rediscovered. Another of these is the confusion which seems to exist (and which has been propagated by a number of recent exhibitions) between Art Deco and *kitsch*. The *kitsch* design of a certain period—the thirties and forties—certainly owes much to Deco, but this is an accident of period. *Kitsch* has no stylistic independence—it vulgarizes other styles, whatever happens to be available at the moment. It is what happens when style falls into the hands of those who have only a

rudimentary notion of stylishness. It is also, often, the result of trying to achieve an "exclusive" effect through the methods of mass production—the conflict between ends and means produces the discord we recognize as *kitsch*.

I have been speaking about the consequences of Art Deco before speaking of its history, which is perhaps the wrong way round. One assumption often made about the style is that it was a reaction against the Art Nouveau which preceded it. A second, linked to this, is that it is an essentially post-World War One development. Neither of these ideas can be sustained. Though Art Nouveau was in many respects a remarkably coherent movement, it reached its peak of success at different times in different parts of Europe. By 1900, at the height of the Belle Epoque, it had already begun to falter; or rather, certain other countries had begun to offer a challenge to the more flowery aspects of Art Nouveau as it had established itself in France.

In 1902, an exhibition of decorative arts was held in Turin. The most important contributions to this were Scottish, Viennese and Italian—that is, they came from designers working at some distance from the centers where Art Nouveau had originally flourished.

From Glasgow came the elongated, angular work of Mackintosh and the MacNairs. Much of the furniture was in black oak; the rest, less forbidding, tended to be painted white, with occasional touches of silver, pink and violet. The Glasgow School showed, as might have been expected, a strong Celtic influence—the characteristic interlacings of Celtic design had, of course, already made a contribution to the Art Nouveau mainstream. But here they were used in an altogether sparer, more stylized fashion. In addition, Mackintosh and his colleagues had felt the impact of the British Arts and Crafts Movement. Indeed, they could be described as the products of that movement, and this meant that they were

V. 'Mᴀᴍ' *Design for a sitting room (Art et Décoration 1914/2–1919). A mixture of oriental, Empire and Louis XV influences can be found in this project.*

corresponding̣ly hostile to Art Nouveau luxuriance and showiness, and favored, instead, the kind of opulence (if opulence there must be) which was·the product of devoted hand craftsmanship. The work of the Glasgow School designers impressed those who saw it in Turin, not only by its originality of proportions and ornament, but by its restraint. The cool, uncluttered feeling had already been propagated in the interiors designed for themselves by Whistler and Wilde; now it became programmatic.

Vienna was represented by artists of the Vienna Secession, and in particular by what was being done in the Wiener Werkstatte under the leadership of the architect Josef Hoffman. The Secession designers had a great sympathy for Mackintosh and his followers, and they were invited to exhibit at the Secession exhibitions in Vienna itself. Hoffman's work, and that of the men he influenced, was even more severe than what had been sent from Glasgow. The Secession was not against

13

the occasional use of intricate pattern, and indeed, in the decorations done by the painter Gustav Klimt for the Palais Stoclet in Brussels, was to be responsible for the last great triumph of Art Nouveau design. But Hoffman himself was attracted to symmetry, to clean-cut simplicity, to rather rigid patterns where pattern was used, and often to rectangular rather than curvilinear shapes.

Finally, there was new design from Italy itself—chairs in parchment on wood, based on egg forms, which were many years ahead of their time; no similar chairs were seen until the 1960's. The designer was Carlo Bugatti (PLATE I), father of the sculptor Rembrandt and the engineer Ettore (who gave the Bugatti name to one of the most famous of all automobiles).

The Turin exhibition was a sign

VI. RUHLMANN. *Design for an alcove (Art et Décoration 1920/1). Even the greatest of the Art Deco cabinet-makers did not despise the problems posed by built-in furniture.*

14

of coming change, but was not a revolution in itself. In Paris, the real home of Art Deco in later years, evolution towards a new style was gradual. People lived, as they always had done, and were to continue to do, in very varied decors. Those with fine Louis XV furniture and houses in the Faubourg St Germain decorated their rooms in traditional style—it is settings of this kind that we must imagine for the grander scenes in Marcel Proust's *Remembrance of Things Past*. Others were content with a clutter of furniture, some clumsy and vulgar and much of it shabby, inherited from their parents and the epoch of the Second Empire. This was how Proust himself lived.

For those with a bit of money to spend, who wanted something new, something as they would have said "original," the established designers produced variations on established Art Nouveau themes. What was chiefly notable was the fact that new kinds of furniture were starting to evolve in response to modern needs—an example is the built-in unit furniture to be seen in PLATE II. But when, in 1905, the Fauves shocked the Parisian public with the violent colors of their paintings—so much so the critics named them the "wild beasts"—there was no corresponding tremor in the world of design. The revolution in fashion and interior decoration had to wait until the Ballets Russes opened their first season in Paris in May 1909.

One ballet in particular captured the imagination of the theater-goers of the time. This was *Shéhérazade*, with Ida Rubinstein as the sultana, Nijinsky as her favorite slave, and a decor by Leon Bakst. Compared to Matisse, the leader of the Fauves, Bakst was a conservative. He was also a man of considerably smaller gifts. Why did his work have such a profound effect? Partly, it was a matter of timing, and the context within which it was seen. The sensuality of Rimsky-Korsakov's music and the splendour of the dancing were

VII. RUHLMANN. *Project for a bedroom (Répertoire du goût Moderne, 1928). This design in mature Art Deco style for a private house should be compared to the foyer of Radio City Music Hall (PLATE 18) which shows similar characteristics.*

put at the service of the orgiastic violence of the story —the ballet ends with a massacre. Violence was in the air, especially among artists and the privileged few. The Italian Futurists, for example, proclaimed at the same epoch that "war is the only hygiene of the world." A fashionable milieu, grown somewhat sick of half-lights, refinements and complications, bored, in fact, with Symbolism and the world of J. K. Huysmans' *A Rebours* (*Against Nature*), responded with excitement to this aspect of the ballet. The fact that Ida Rubinstein was not a professional dancer, but a beautiful society woman who had taken to the stage, gave *Shéhérazade* additional piquancy.

Bakst's decor, though a new departure in its opulence of color, was not entirely revolutionary. A St. Petersburg Symbolist who had absorbed a good many lessons from Aubrey Beardsley (whose work was well-known in Russia at this time) offered a highly spiced version of a familiar dish. The color was as much generically Russian as personal; we see the same kind of sensibility at work in the glowing hues and strange color-juxtapositions of Russian icons. But both costumes and settings struck an immediate chord with those who saw them—a new dream, and therefore a new style, were born as a result.

The effect on clothes was that they became freer, gauzier and sexier. The couturier of the moment was Paul Poiret—when Poiret's rival, Jean Worth, saw the pantaloon dresses the former was bringing in, he called them "vulgar, wicked and ugly." But a whiff of sinfulness was just what women wanted. In 1912, Poiret sold a million francs' worth of clothes on the first day's showing of his new collection. Interior decoration was orientalized—also partly under Poiret's aegis. In 1911 he opened his own decorating business, under the name of Martine. Seat furniture became lower to allow for the languorous attitudes and gestures modelled on Rubinstein. Strong colors were in favor; lighting was dimmed and diffused; cushions were everywhere; extensive use was made of pattern-on-pattern (Bakst was a master of this kind of effect). PLATES III to VI give an excellent idea of the fashionable decoration inspired by the Ballets Russes, a style which spanned the best part of a decade, including the whole period of the First World War.

Of course, "pure" orientalism soon turned out to be impractical. Points to notice in these settings are the intrusion of elements other than eastern ones. The couch in PLATE III, for example, is a revival of a Directoire model, but with lower legs and in consequence a higher curve of the back to balance them. Similarly, the spoon-backed chair in the center of PLATE IV is based on the *chaise gondole* of about 1800. Low seats required lower tables to match, as can be seen in PLATE V. This is the epoch

VIII. PAUL FOLLOT. *Chest in sycamore, ebony and silvered bronze (Art et Décoration 1922/1). Shows the strong Louis XVI influence in much Art Deco design.*

which saw the birth of that ubiquitous piece, the cocktail table. The interest in built-in furniture continued, as can also be seen in PLATE VI. One reason for this, apart from the fact that the war and its aftermath forced people to live in smaller spaces, is that pattern, color and texture—in other words fabrics and wallpapers—came, in the more oriental types of decor, to dominate form. Furniture was simplified, so as to fade into the background. Much of it—the squashy cushions and divans—could scarcely be said to have "form" at all.

The war naturally administered a check to the development of fashion, and especially of fashions in interior decoration, which remained more or less frozen for the duration of the conflict. This was not true of art. The war-time years were those which saw the development of Analytic and Synthetic Cubism. Unknown to all but a very few in Paris, the Dada Movement was born in Zurich. This was to be a prime source for the Surrealism which dominated avant-garde thinking in Paris from the early Twenties onwards. De Stijl, also rife with consequences for the future, was founded in Holland in 1917, and it was in this year that Rietveld designed his famous angular all-wood chair—one of the first examples of all-out "modernism" in furniture.

What happened in France when peace came? It is sometimes alleged, even now, that the war had a liberating effect on society, and that Art Deco is the expression of the jazz age which followed the armistice. It is true that the twenties are rightly remembered as *Les Années Folles*—people claimed the right to live as they pleased, to discard the old social and moral conventions. The parties described by Scott Fitzgerald undoubtedly took place, fancy dress balls were

IX. *Entry to the boutique of the couturière Jeanne Lanvin, designed by A-A Rateau. This designer was strongly influenced by the ancient world. The designs on the lift-cage are almost Minoan.*

X. EILEEN GRAY. *Another interior designed for Suzanne Talbot (L'Illustration—27.5.33). Superb simplicity was the hallmark of Eileen Gray's work.*

given (but Poiret had given them too—300 people drank 900 bottles of champagne at his memorable "Persian Celebration" in 1911), people gave rein to a slightly hysterical gaiety. Some things, of course, were permanently changed. There was a new atmosphere of informality to be savored at places such as Cocteau's bar *Le Boeuf sur le Toit,* where socialites mingled with artists—but even this could be described as a tamed and civilized successor to the wild Futurist cabarets run by members of the avant-garde in Moscow, just before the war, and in Zurich during it.

In Paris, there was a dance craze—the Charleston, the black-bottom, the one-step, the fox-trot, the shimmy and the tango. There was a craze for things American too, and especially for American Negroes. Josephine Baker electrified Paris in 1925, in the *Revue Nègre.* There was a vogue for the outdoor life. Women, in particular, after shutting themselves up in

XI. EILEEN GRAY. *Interior designed
for Suzanne Talbot (L'Illustration—
27.5.33). The spectacular interiors
of this apartment were the nearest
Art Deco got to true modernism.
Note the Japanese screen,
archaeological objects and African
stool.*

the harem, came out and took to the beach. Diaghilev, the impresario who had presented *Shéhérazade,* now mounted a ballet called *Le Train Bleu* (1924), to show off a new English dancer called Anton Dolin. Diaghilev got the idea when he saw Dolin doing handstands at Monte Carlo. The costumes were bathing costumes, golfing clothes and a tennis dress, and they were the work of the couturière of the moment, Coco Chanel. Women, having tasted a new kind of physical freedom during the war, were not going to surrender it, and Chanel's abbreviated clothes, with their short skirts, bare arms and low waistlines, were the symbol of this determination.

Underneath it all, however, and especially among those who had survived the war with their money intact, there was a profound sense of shock. Shock, in turn, bred a kind of caution. Even amongst the artists of the avant-garde, there was a momentary tendency to draw back. In 1921, Picasso created the last of his

Synthetic Cubist masterpieces, *The Three Musicians*. He had, however, already begun to experiment with a revival of neo-classicism, and these handsome neo-classical works were characteristic of his production in the early twenties. Matisse had withdrawn to the South of France in 1917, and had eventually settled in Nice, where he was to remain for the rest of his life. He began work on the long series of hedonistic paintings, mostly showing women in interiors, which were to preoccupy him until the Second World War.

Art Deco was now the established fashion among people who liked to think of themselves as taste-makers. It was to reach a culminating point in the Exposition des Arts Décoratifs of 1925, which had originally been planned for 1914, and which gave the style its generally accepted name, and was to decline and be progressively watered down thereafter. The principal patrons were neither the avant-garde (who were too poor, as were the leading intellectuals), nor the possessors of "old" money—aristocratic and mercantile fortunes—though a few fashionable artistocrats did provide commissions. At first, in the best period of Deco, they were people involved with the mode and modishness. Among them were the couturière, Jeanne Lanvin, who commissioned Albert-Armand Rateau to decorate her house in the rue Barbet-de-Jouy and her boutique in the Faubourg St. Honoré; her rival, Madeleine Vionnet, who filled her house with lacquer by Jacques Dunand; and a

XIII. *Jacques Doucet's sitting-room, rue St. James, Neuilly (L'Illustration—Mai 1930). Note the large sofa by Marcel Coard, with a painting by the Douanier Rousseau hanging above it.*

third dress-designer, Jacques Doucet.

In this context, Doucet is an especially fascinating figure. He had originally been a collector of eighteenth century pictures and furniture. He wearied of these, and sold them at auction in 1912; then immediately set about furnishing his new home in the avenue du Bois, and later his apartment in the rue St. James with works by the post-Impressionists, and later with Cubist paintings and sculpture, and work by the Surrealists (André Breton, leader of the Surrealist Movement, advised him). To these contemporary works he added examples of African, Chinese and Islamic art. The setting for his collections was created by the leading names in Art Deco: Pierre Legrain, Clément Rousseau, Eileen Gray, Rose Adler, Marcel Coard, Gustave Miklos, André Groult and René Lalique. In the Neuilly apartment, built in 1927, and illustrated in PLATES XII, XIII and XIV,

XIV. Entrance to Jacques Doucet's apartment in Neuilly. The carpet is by Marcoussis, the stair-rail is by Josef Csaky, and the sculpture of the stair-landing is "Mlle Pogany" by Brancusi.

there was a parquet floor by Legrain, a metal staircase by Josef Csaky, carpets by Louis Marcoussis, Jean Lurçat and by Miklos. It was the last of the great Art Deco interiors created for a private client. Doucet died in 1929, the year of the Wall Street crash, and so did Legrain and (for that matter) Diaghilev.

The photographs of Doucet's apartment make an interesting study today. PLATE XIII, for instance, shows, on the left, an immense ivory inlaid sofa by Coard, which recently appeared at auction in Paris, and which now holds the auction record for a piece of Art Deco furniture. Hanging above it is a masterpiece by the Douanier Rousseau, *The Snake Charmer*. Also visible is a group of Cubist paintings and a sculptured head by Modigliani. PLATE XIV shows the staircase by Csaky. On the half-landing is a head by Brancusi, the *Portrait of Mlle Pogany*.

These pictures give a strong impression of the refinement of Doucet's taste and the luxury with which he surrounded himself. But the arrangement of the rooms is relatively conventional, and there is nothing here which could pass either as an expression of a new technology, or, indeed, as a genuine piece of twentieth century industrial design. These are wonderful expressions of the will to style, embodiments of the dream I have described, but each detail has been individually created by a craftsman. In this respect, Doucet's apartment is the direct descendant of the *petits appartements* created for Louis XV and Louis XVI at Versailles.

At first sight, the apartment designed by Eileen Gray for Suzanne Talbot (Mme Mathieu Lévy), has a more radical look (PLATES X and XI). Miss Gray created a wonderfully dramatic setting for her client by combining satiny white walls and a silvered matt glass floor, which was illuminated from below. But in fact many elements tell us that the family resemblance to

XV. Decoration for the Normandie. Panel by Dupas; lacquer by Dunand (Art et Décoration Juillet 1933). Art Deco becomes an official style.

Bauhaus design to be found in some details, such as the armchairs with their metal frames, is a deceptive one. The basic feeling is still oriental, though the violent Bakst colors have been bleached away. The low divans are still there, the patterned cushions have been replaced by zebra and leopard skins, and furs. A two-leaf Japanese screen (screens of this type are the ultimate source of the kind of wall decoration to be seen in PLATE IV) is placed behind the divan; flanking it are a pair of Egyptian canopic jars. The African stools are the genuine article—Doucet had adaptations made for him by Legrain (PLATES XII and XIII). What is fascinating here, as with the Doucet apartment, is the statement it makes about the owner

and her preferred life-style. It is a portrait of Mlle Talbot composed by the designer.

XVI. *Detail from decoration for the Normandie. Panel by Jean Dupas (L'Illustration Juin 1935).*

It is in looking at illustrations such as these that one begins to understand the description given by Jacques Chastenet of the 1925 exhibition. He speaks of:

> Pure white spattered with brilliant splashes; orgies of lacquer; furniture deliberately rigid, made in rare woods and sometimes covered with shagreen; textiles and wallpapers either blinding like the decor of one of the earliest Russian ballets, or as chaste as a drawing-board diagram; panels with drily geometric outlines and field painted with convolvulus and frolicking

27

sea-horses; trinkets in precious materials; smoked crystal; negro masks; paintings on which all the ardour of the young schools was released; effervescent luminous cascades.

However, there is not much, if indeed anything, in this description, which could be applied to one isolated section—the pavilion *L'Esprit Nouveau,* designed by Le Corbusier. The architect had a great deal of trouble with the exhibition authorities, who alloted him the worst site at their disposal, and then proceeded to build a fence eighteen feet high round the structure, to keep any possible visitors out. This was eventually torn down when a cabinet minister was asked to intervene on the architect's behalf. Both the structure itself—an early example of "system" building—and its contents were in total opposition to the rest of the show. What they expressed, however imperfectly (for Corbusier's furniture tends to look factory-made while being unsuitable to mass production) was faith in a future dominated by the machine, and therefore, in consequence, by a machine aesthetic.

Whatever influences Art Deco itself absorbed from modern art (and as I have said it did absorb some, though fewer from modern architecture) it remained committed to very different ideals. The cabinet by Paul Follot which appears in PLATE VIII is a case in point. The shape of this piece is pure Louis XVI, and the mounts and feet are both related to eighteenth century models. But it is not a copy. Slight changes have been made in the proportions, and the materials used—sycamore, ebony and silvered bronze—locate the piece firmly in the early twenties. Until recently, a piece of this type would have been dismissed out of hand as an example of "Louis the hotel"—it is the conservative, rather than the radical, aspect of Art Deco which people have found it hardest to understand and appreciate, and which has therefore been slowest to return to favor. But it is possible to regard furniture of this sort as something which makes a logical, and in the circumstances of the time, wholly understandable, statement about traditional values, and the need to support these in the post-war chaos. It is significant to note the more-than-accidental resemblances to be discovered between some of the Deco furniture of the Twenties, and the furniture produced under Louis XVIII and Charles X—in the epoch the French call *Restoration*. In this, too, one discovers an innate conservatism of form, a contrasting originality of color and decoration and a deeply satisfying perfection of workmanship.

XVII. *Interior of the Normandie. Large Salon (L'Illustration Juin 1935). This drawing gives a good idea of the kind of public the Normandie was meant to cater to. Note the typically Art Deco forms of the free-standing light-fittings.*

After the crash of 1929, Art Deco survived largely through official, rather than private patronage. France itself, with its balanced economy based upon agriculture, suffered a great deal less than the more heavily industrialized nations from the economic stringencies of the time. Many Frenchmen were not sorry to see the Ritz bar again become a piece of French, rather than American, territory. But the little world of successful couturiers and their allies no longer felt secure. The fashion for redecoration, rather than an indulgence in entirely new architectural ventures (itself a commentary on the post-war situation) became, if not too expensive, then too ostentatious for the times.

Attitudes were different where national prestige was involved. When the liner *Normandie* was fitted out in 1935, it was intended to be a demonstration of the very best that French craftsmen could create. The environment was to be the *neplus ultra* of its kind, just as the first-class restaurant was to represent the perfection of French cooking. The best craftsmen were employed—Dunand provided giant murals, so did artists such as J-C Domergue, Jean Dupas (PLATE XV), Paul Jouve and Max Ingrand. The bathrooms were lined with ceramic tiles by Jean Mayodon; the furniture was by Jules Leleu and Alavoine among others; there was wrought iron by Subes and there were textiles by Rodier. An artist's impression of the large salon (PLATE XVII) shows the general effect all this was intended to produce; and it gives a good idea, too, of the kind of people who were supposed to take advantage of the luxury the ship offered—a vision of a world in which every man is as handsome as a film-star, and every woman as well turned out as a millionaire's mistress.

In the *Normandie's* interiors, and especially in the ship's public rooms, Art Deco was on the way to discovering its second destiny—not as actual luxury for the few, but as the illusion of luxury for the many. We find it fulfilling this role not so much in France as in the grandiose interiors of Radio City, which ante-date the *Normandie* itself by two years. On a less ambitious scale, the designers of the chain of Odeon cinemas built in England in the thirties made use of Art Deco ideas and conventions, with the same end in view—that of heightening the visitor's sense of well-being, and of making him feel that he had found his way into a more glamorous realm. The illusion was heightened by many of the films he saw there—films like the Rogers-Astaire musicals, where the sets were full of Deco touches. It would, nevertheless, be a mistake to confuse this Hollywood idea of Deco, though often executed with the utmost polish, with the real thing as it flourished in France.

It is worthwhile, for example, to compare the Radio City interior (PLATE XVIII) with the project for a bedroom by the great French designer and cabinet-maker Ruhlmann (PLATE VII), especially as they are close to one another in date. Despite the difference in

XVIII. *Radio City, New York (Art et Décoration Avril 1933).*
Ruhlmann's decorative ideas have here been exported across the Atlantic, and reproduced on a monumental scale.

function, a number of common characteristics emerge. We note, to choose the most conspicuous of these, the over-scale cylindrical lighting fixtures which are such a prominent feature in each case. We note, too, the use of regular vertical emphases, long curtains falling from cornice to floor. In each case, these rhythmic verticals are contradicted by a low-set horizontal—the gallery at Radio City, the vast low bed in the Ruhlmann project. In each, too, there is an almost exaggerated feeling of space—such furniture as there is is pushed back against the walls.

Yet the feeling they give is different. The Ruhlmann bedroom is refined, understated; the Radio City interior is grandiose and rather coarse in detail. One murmurs; the other shouts. Once the Deco style, invented for a small and fastidious clientèle, was projected to the mass public, it slowly lost its identity.

At the same time, the more superficial aspects of the style began to permeate the household goods produced for the mass market. The 'jazz' patterns of lodging-house carpets and railway upholstery; the fan-shaped wall-lights in the hallways of thirties apartment blocks; much of the decorative pottery and glass still to be found in department stores—all these represent the kind of "no taste" that Art Deco became as it spread outwards and became available to everybody. We are still so much conditioned to the worst aspects of the movement that it is hard to appreciate the best.

Yet that best has remained potent—not merely because we now again recognize it as a valid expression of the age and of the people who created it, but because it continues to permeate our way of thinking. Designers have come up with new ideas about furniture, just as painters have come up with new ideas about painting. But, curiously enough, nobody has come up with a new notion of luxury. Ebony and ivory, shagreen and leather, lacquer and enamel—Art Deco imposed itself permanently on our imaginations, not only through decorative forms, but through the textures and colors it associated with itself. It had the courage of its convictions, and that, most of all, is the thing which makes it potent.

PLATE 2

PLATE

PLATE
(OVERLEA

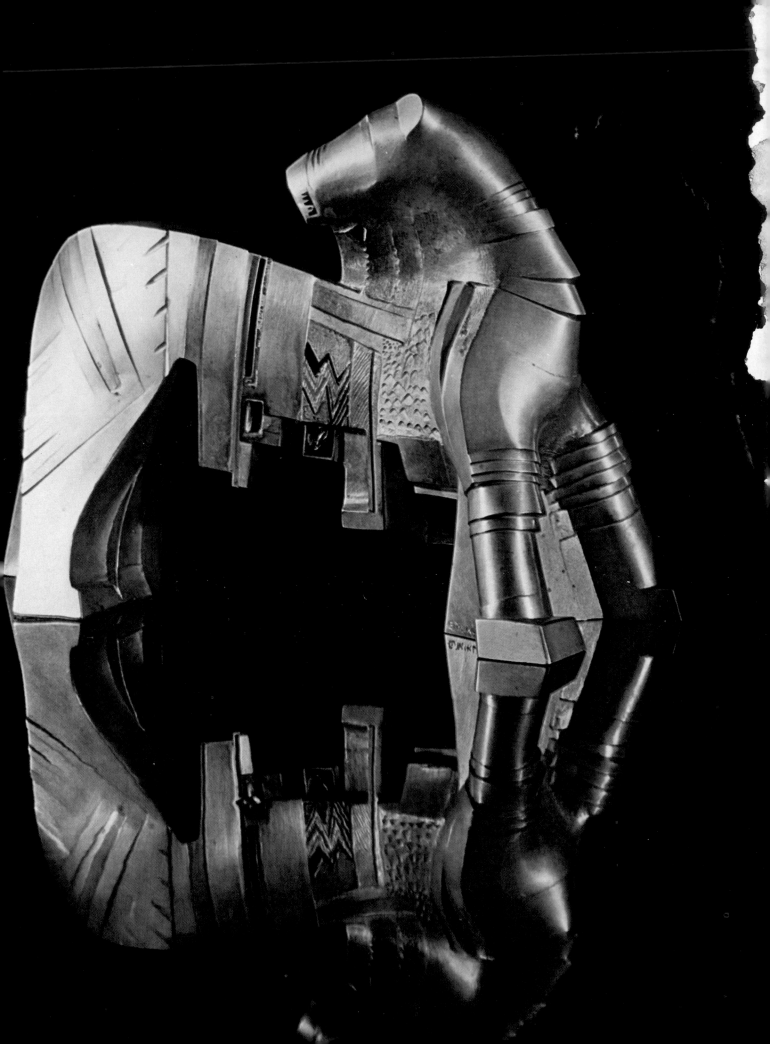

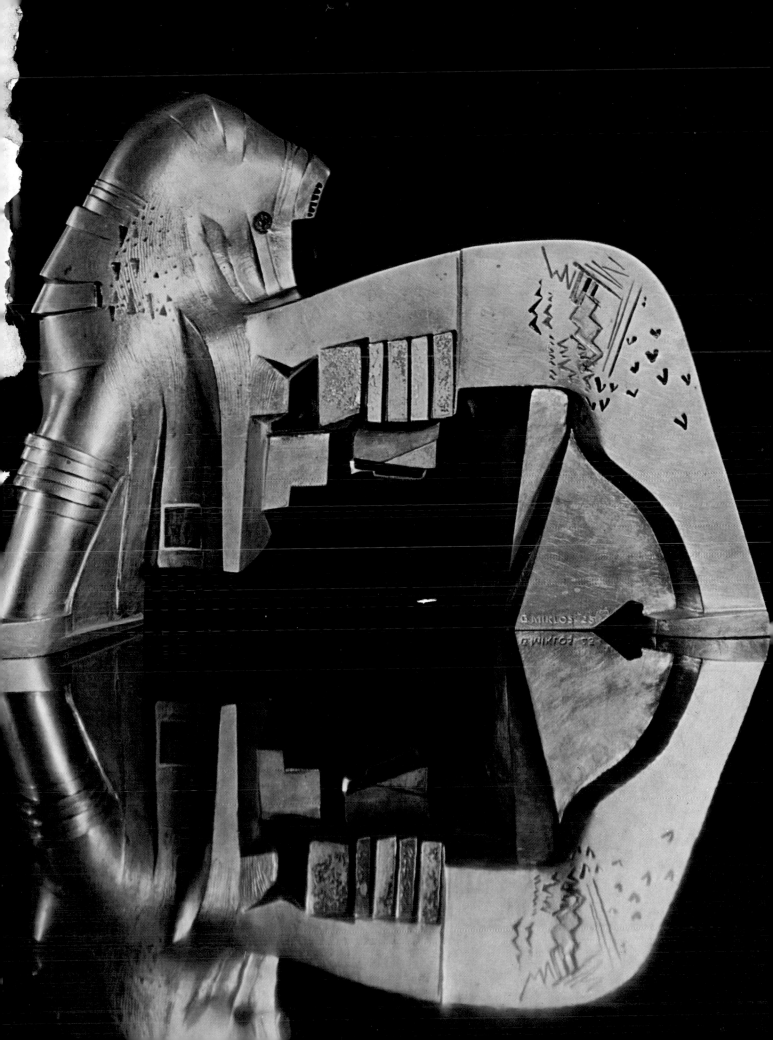

PLATE 6

PLATE 7

PLATE 5

PLATE 8 (OVERLEAF)

PLATE 13

PLATE 14

LATE 15

PLATE 16

PLATE 17A

PLATE 17B

PLATE 18

1. ROGER DE LA FRESAYNE, Man with a pipe, *Water color on paper. 1917.*

2. TAMARA DE LEMPICKA, The Musician, *Oil on canvas, dated 1929. A Polish artist who painted personalities of the twenties and thirties in a style typical of the period.*

3. FRANCOIS-LOUIS SCHMIED and JEAN DUNAND, *Lizard skin and lacquer binding for the Comtesse de Noaille's* Climats.
Schmied published books for members of the Bibliophilic Society. For the luxurious bindings he used plaques in lacquer, enamel and precious metals. These were designed by Dunand, Goulden and Miklos.

4. GUSTAV MIKLOS, Four dogs in gilt bronze and colored metals, *Dated 1925.*
Formerly in the Douchet collection. Exhibited Jacques Douchet, Meubles 1925 Musee des Arts Decoratifs, Paris 1961. Most of Douchet's furniture is now in this museum.

5. EMILE-JACQUES RUHLMANN, Writing Cabinet, *Part of a suite of Caucasian burr walnut.*
Plaque in silver bronze attributed to Jannoit. The wood was brought over the Caucasian mountains on men's backs and exchanged for gold ingots.

6. FRANÇOIS-EMILE DECORCHEMONT, Group of Vases.
Decorchement was a leading glass maker who used the technique called Pâte-de-verre. Each piece has the artist's stamp and often an engraved number.

7. FRANÇOIS-EMILE DECORCHEMONT, Vases.

8. JEAN DUNAND, Vases, *Lacquer. Dunand was considered by contemporary critics to be the greatest craftsman of his age. He revived the difficult techniques of Japanese lacquer.*

9. GABRIEL ARGY-ROUSSEAU, Vases and box.
Exhibited by the artist at the Salons des Artistes Décorateurs. These objects, made in series, are of fine quality.

10. RENÈ LALIQUE, Vases, *Moulded glass. Lalique was originally famous as an art nouveau jeweller and goldsmith. He used colored glass pastes in his brooches and pendants during the 1890's. He then experimented with blown glass, but little has survived. After the war, his factory in Wingen-sur-Moden began to make the moulded glass which has become associated with his name.*

11. MAURICE MARINOT, Bottle, *crystal.*

12. JEAN DUNAND, Vase, *Lacquer on metal.*
Dunand learned the technique of lacquer on metal work from the Japanese, Sugawara. Initially he used it to enhance the metal base, and not as a fundamental part of the decoration as on this vase. The balance of the spheres against the rectangular support, perhaps, owe something to Dunand's training as a sculptor.

13. JEAN DUNAND, Lacquer panel.
After the First World War, Dunand opened workshops in the rue Hallè, where he employed as many as a hundred workmen, among them Indo-Chinese, who were less prone to the skin allergy lacquer can cause. The workshop made furniture, decorative panels and screens, as well as vases, boxes and cigarette cases.

14. JEAN DUNAND, Lacquer panel.

15. EDOUARD BENEDICTUS, Carpet.
Benedictus started as a book binder. Later he published three collections of textile design, Variations, Nouvelle Variations *and* Relais. *His cartoon for carpets and tapestries was executed by the Aubusson factory.*

16. CAMILLE FAURÉ, Vases, *Limoges enamel.*
Limoges has been a center of enamel making for centuries, but by 1900 the work produced was a mere pastiche of the 16th century design. Fauré gave new life to the factory with his pearlized, brilliantly colored vases decorated with geometric designs, which were produced between 1924 and 1936.

17A and 17B. CAMILLE FAURÉ, Limoges enamel.

18. JEAN DUNAND, Ibis, *Gold and red lacquer panel, 1931.*
A preparatory panel for decoration in the liner Atlantique, *which was lost in a fire. The birds are realistic, but the background suggests op art. Exhibited in Munich at the Exhibition of the Olympic Games, 1972.*

19. T-L. Madrazo, The Street,
Gouache on paper. 1926
Many post-war artists depicted the
contemporary underworld. Exhibited in
Minneapolis Institute of Art, 1971.

1   PAINTING

The painters whose work can be identified with the Art Deco style, and who collaborated in some of the principal Art Deco projects, form a curious sub-group, or, rather, a whole series of sub-groups, within the main pattern of the art of the time. None of these artists were major innovators, and none played any particularly decisive part in the development of what we now call the Ecole de Paris—that amalgamation of native French artists (such men as Braque and Léger) and others who were French only by adoption (Picasso, Juan Gris, Chagall, Ernst, Soutine). It was the men of the Ecole de Paris who made what was happening in France the cynosure of Europe. The men to be discussed here had, for the most part, more modest ambitions. It was their ability to adapt themselves to the demands of an overall decorative scheme which brought them success.

Inevitably, many of the artists identified with the Art Deco style also show the influence of Modernism, and particularly, as we shall see, of Cubism. But they tended to make an eclectic and often rather frivolous use of Cubist conventions, just as, for example, an artist such as Erté plundered Persian and Indian miniatures, as well as Japanese prints and Indonesian textiles, for the best of their decorative effects. The unspoken assumption was that the individuality of the artist remained subordinate to the demands of the overall stylistic concept.

In this sense, the painters whose work is associated with Art Deco continued a tradition which had been created when Art Nouveau was the dominant mode. When we try to focus, in the mind's eye, the essential qualities and themes of Art Nouveau, it is decorative details, not paintings as such, that come to mind. Indeed, while one can think of numerous painters whose work fed the development of Art Nouveau—men such as Burne-Jones and Gustave Moreau—it is hard to think of artists of any stature who can be labelled "typically Art Nouveau," without any further word of explanation. Even Beardsley, whose illustrations spread the gospel of the *fin de siècle* style throughout Europe, from St. Petersburg to Barcelona, transcends Art Nouveau conventions—so too do Fernand Khnopff and Gustav Klimt, though their work incorporates many details which refer directly to the ideas which Art Nouveau decorators and craftsmen also tried to express.

Similarly, we must think of the fine arts, painting and sculpture, as things which played a subordinate, rather than a traditionally dominant, part in the creation of the Art Deco environment.

The best defined and most immediately recognizable and identifiable group of Art Deco artists were the animal painters. These men were the heirs of the Romantic Movement in painting. Many of the greatest of the Romantic artists—Delacroix and Géricault, for example—had been obsessed with animals, horses and the larger felines in particular, as symbols of the savage forces at work in the world and at work, too, within their own unbridled temperaments. Somewhat later in the nineteenth century, certain artists, less great but nevertheless men of considerable talent, had made reputations as specialists in animal painting. Among the best known were Barye (even more celebrated for his animal sculptures) and Rosa Bonheur.

The animal painters of the nineteenth century always painted their subjects as an integral part of the surrounding landscape. This is not the case with their Art Deco successors. Artists such as Paul Jouve, Jacques Nam and André Margat cede nothing to their predecessors in terms of observation. The wonderful keenness of Jouve's eye can be savoured in a whole group of illustrations in this book. But we immediately notice, too, the way in which he and the others I have named tend to treat their animals as decorative silhouettes, placed against a ground which isolates the form and emphasizes the completeness of the bounding outline.

Among the animals most in favor with these artists were felines of all kinds—ranging from domestic cats to panthers, leopards, lions and tigers—and also snakes and elephants. The felines and the snakes were traditional—inherited from the Romantics in the case of the former, and from Symbolism and Art Nouveau in the case of the latter. But it is interesting to note how the powerful emotional overtones which earlier artists had given to these creatures were avoided by the new generation of artists. With Jouve's panthers, we are aware not only of the silhouette, but of the powerful faceted forms which the artist discovers beneath the pelt (PLATES 25, 26 and 27). The animal becomes a kind of emblem of the more striking aspects of Art Deco luxury.

In the same fashion Art Deco snakes are used in a neutral way, for the sake of their glittering scales and that of the rhythmic curves suggested by the form of the reptile, and not as symbols of lust and evil. One notes that it was at this period that reptile skin became ultra-fashionable for wear as shoes, belts and handbags.

The interest in elephants was something newer. In part, it may have sprung from the fact that Art Deco craftsmen had a passion for ivory. But largely it seems to have been due to the French involvement in Indo-China. Elephants became particularly fashionable at the time of the great Colonial Exhibition in 1931. The specimen to be seen in PLATE 22, which is also the work of Jouve, will suggest yet a third reason for this fascination with the massive beasts—the fact that their monumental proportions, when viewed from certain angles, provided a kind of equivalent of forms which, reduced to abstract terms, already fascinated contemporary designers.

The specialists in animals were to some extent protected, by the nature of their speciality, from the seductions of Modernism. But Modernism did, nevertheless, have its impact on the Art Deco environment. This happened in two ways. In the first place, a number of artists who were undoubtedly Modernist ventured into the field of design—thus we find ceramics decorated by Matisse, Vlaminck, van Dongen and Dufy; textile designs by Dufy and Laurencin; tapestries by Lurçat Rouault, Léger, Derain and Braque; rugs by Lurçat and Marcoussis. When they ventured into the field of decoration and the applied arts, these distinguished painters often came up with a result which had a vaguely Art Deco look.

In the second place, there were artists who, while basically they were not innovative, found in post-Impressionist and Cubist work a source of decorative ideas. Two of the most inventive of these were the sculptors Miklos and Csaky, who also produced some attractive gouaches (PLATES 29 and 30). Madrazo's drawing *The Street*, which is rather less successful (PLATE 19) is nevertheless interesting because it shows the uneven way in which Modernist influences were absorbed. The idea stems from Lautrec, the male figure owes something to Picasso's paintings of the Blue Period, and the female is a salute to Modigliani. The background seems to be cribbed by Delaunay's Eiffel Tower paintings.

Even pure abstraction, of the type pioneered by Kandinsky, could on occasion be pressed into service, as can be seen from the two asbestos panels by Lagarde (PLATES 31 and 32). These are dated 1926, which places them some sixteen years later than Kandinsky's first "abstract improvisations" and gives some notion of the kind of time-lag required for the world of fashion to assimilate the more difficult modernist ideas.

The division between the Art Deco decorative painters and the Modernists was not of course absolute, as we have already seen in considering the decorative work done by a number of painters of the Ecole de Paris. Certain artists managed to keep a foot in both camps, among them the elegant Japanese Foujita (PLATE 35), and Marie Laurencin, whose paintings of young girls, enclosed in frames made of strips of mirror, hung in many of the smartest twenties drawing-rooms.

Indeed, Laurencin and Matisse between them created the formula for a new type of decorative picture, exemplified here by the *Head of a Girl* by Jean Dupas (PLATE 37), an artist much favored by the great decorator and cabinet-maker Jacques-Emile Ruhlmann, who made a work by Dupas one of the focal points of his exhibit in the 1925 exhibition. The freshest and most attractive work done in a recognizably Deco idiom is, however, the work of fashion, theater and poster designers, and book illustrators.

The arrival of the Russian ballet in 1909 naturally influenced not only theater design—the work of Erté, (PLATES 47 and 48) for instance, is scarcely imaginable without the initial impulse supplied by Bakst—but also the fashion illustrators of the day, among them the delightful Georges Lepape. PLATE 35, a charming specimen of his work, shows how the sultana of *Shéhérazade* could be translated into the demurer style demanded by fashion magazines such as the *Gazette du Bon Ton* and *Fémina*, which were launched about the time that Diaghilev and his dancers arrived in Paris.

The work of Lepape and his colleagues was essentially eclectic. They borrowed ideas wherever it suited them—from Japanese prints (PLATES 33, 38, 40 show Lepape producing a European equivalent of the large heads of geishas typical of the great Japanese printmaker Utamaro), from their own contemporaries (PLATE 43 is a very competent popularization of ideas borrowed from Pascin), from the newly fashionable Persian miniatures, then just becoming available to rich Parisian collectors such as Doucet.

Book illustrations tend to be more luxurious and considered versions of the style which was used in the fashion magazines—linear, with fat washes of color, and hatched shading. Woodcuts were popular, because these characteristics were in any case typical of the woodcut medium. Jouve made a famous set of illustrations for Kipling's *Jungle Book,* published in a French translation by F-L Schmied in 1917—these were turned into woodblocks, some of which were cut by the artist himself.

The list of talented book illustrators is quite a long one—in addition to Jouve and Lepape, it includes Charles Martin, Guy Arnoux, Benito, Barbier Robert Bonfils, Brunnelleschi, Alberto Lorenzi, Charles Martin, André Edouard Marty, André Dignimont, J-E Laboureur, Charles Laborde, Jean-Louis Boussingault, Paul Véra, Drésa, Jean Dupas and the multi-faceted Paul Iribe. The illustrations themselves tend to have three main themes: an eighteenth century dream-world, with pierrots and columbines, powdered wigs and crinolines; depictions of the "modern woman," heavily stylized and romanticized; and scenes from fashionable life, to which may be added scenes from low-life —the smart world of the twenties had a certain *nostalgie de la boue.*

The pictures often formed part of a larger and more important artistic whole, as the period saw a steady production of luxurious limited editions. Publishers such as Kieffer, Piazza, Schmied and the Beltrand brothers produced books which were fine specimens of the printer's and binder's crafts. Binders were well patronized. The subscriber to a particular book —and most limited editions of this type were financed by means of a subscription list—could of course choose his own binding. These were made in colored leathers, heightened with gold, silver or platinum tooling, and most of the time adorned with lacquer or enamel plaques, by men such as Dunand, Goulden or Miklos.

Among the most important bookbinders of the twenties were Pierre Legrain, Rose Adler, and Dunand, all of whom worked for Jacques Doucet, who had a famous library. Other binders, or designers of bindings, were Paul Bonet, Robert Bonfils, René Kieffer, Georges Crette, and the most important of all, F-L Schmied. Designs for book-bindings were also made by furniture designers, such as André Mare and Clément Mère. The bindings became the significant work of art, rather than the book itself.

The art of the poster, which had flourished so exceedingly during the nineties, survived into the post-war period. The best of those produced in the twenties are theatrical. Often particular artists became associated with particular stars, as Mucha had been associated with Sarah Bernhardt. Charles Gesmar, a Rumanian artist who died at the age of 28, put Mistinguett's smile on every *colonne d'affiche* in Paris. He also designed posters for the Dolly Sisters, for Jane Marnac, and for the transvestite acrobat, Barbette, who was so much admired by Jean Cocteau. Paul Colin was the first to spot the potential of the

American dancer Josephine Baker, who caused a sensation in 1925, when she appeared in the *Revue Nègre* clad in nothing but a bunch of bananas. Colin also made a fine poster for the jazz players Wiener and Doucet, who were the big attractions of Cocteau's *Le Boeuf sur le Toit*.

In the commercial field, some of the most striking work was done by Jean Carlu and by Cassandre (Adolphe-Jean-Marie Mouton). Their bold "Cubist" graphics gave the subject-matter an immediately recognizable image, even if the poster was merely glimpsed from a speeding car. Carlu's *Dentrifice Gelé* and *Paris-Soir,* and Cassandre's *Etoile du Nord* and *Dubonnet* mark a turning point in the history of poster-advertising: the birth of hard-sell.

20. ROGER DE LA FRESNAYE, The Clarinetist, *Water color on paper, Dated 1917.*
De la Fresnaye was a pupil of the Nabia Sérusier and Maurice Denis, exhibited with the Cubists, though his work is generally more conservative and more consciously decorative than theirs. This water color is one of a series intended for the illustration of a book by Jean Cocteau, which was never published.

21. (OVERLEAF)
ROGER DE LA FRESNAYE, The Guitarist, *Water color on paper, 1917. Same series.*

20

21

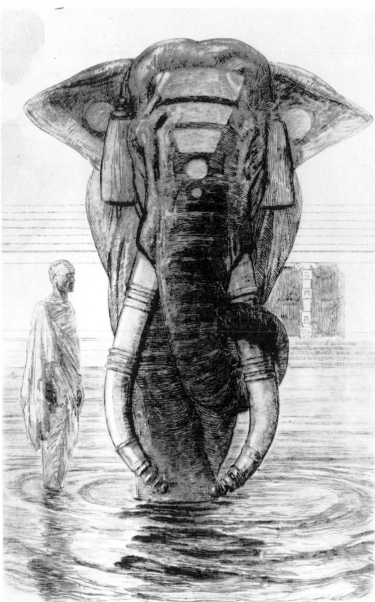

22

22. PAUL JOUVE, The Elephant,
Lithograph.
*Jouve exhibited his first animal picture
at the Salon National when he was 15.
He studied wild beasts in captivity in
the zoos of Europe, but went as far as
Angkor to draw elephants in their
natural surroundings. This print is
related in style to the painting shown
at the Colonial Exhibition at Vincennes.*

23. PAUL JOUVE, Panther and Boa
constrictor, *Lithograph on silk.
Numbered 2/2.*
*One of Jouve's best known works is the
Livre de la Jungle, published by
Schmied in 1917. Jouve only
completed 15 of the 90 wood blocks;
Schmied engraved the others from the
artist's sketches.*

23

24

25

24. PAUL JOUVE, Panther in a Tree, *Water color on paper*.

25. PAUL JOUVE, Walking Panther, *Lithograph. Numbered 6/50.*
Jouve showed at the Gallerie Georges Petit in Paris from 1921 onwards, together with the lacquerer Jean Dunand, the silversmith and enameller, Jean Goulden, and the book designer/ engraver and publisher Schmied.

26. PAUL JOUVE, Panther, *Water color on paper*.

27. PAUL JOUVE, Panther with his Prey, *Water color on paper*.

26

27

28. Paul JOUVE, *Two Walking Tigers,*
Water color on paper.

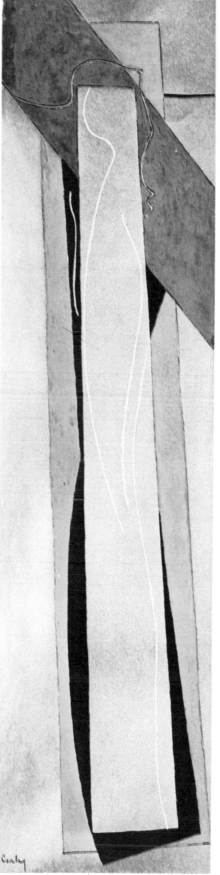

29. GUSTAV MIKLOS, Clown, *Gouache on paper, dated 1920.*
Miklos was best known as a sculptor. He studied painting in his native Budapest before coming to Paris in 1909. He exhibited at the Salon des Independants.

30. JOSEF CSAKY, Human form, *Gouache on paper, 1920.*
Like Miklos, Csaky was primarily a sculptor. His sensitive semi-abstract figures in stone or bronze place him in the main stream of Cubism.

30

31. M. LAGARDE, *Gouache on asbestos dated 1926.*
Modernism had only a belated influence on the decorative arts, which lagged some 10 to 12 years behind Cubist and Abstract experiments.

32. M. LAGARDE, *Gouache on asbestos.*

32

33

33. GEORGES LEPAPE, Spring, *Gouache on paper. 1927.*

34. FOUJITA, The Lovers, *Gouache on paper, signed and dated in Japanese 1917.*
Foujita designed wallpapers and textiles in addition to producing the well-known portraits of himself and his friends, and his cats.

35. GEORGES LEPAPE, Moonlight, *Gouache on paper.*
In the interiors designed by Martine, the firm run by Poiret, cushions often replaced the seats. This was considered particularly daring.

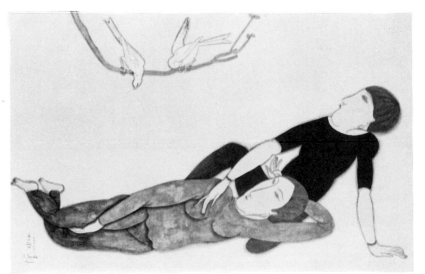

34

35

37

36. EUGENE ROBERT POUGHEON, The Riderless Horse, *Pencil on paper. Pougheon won academic honors – The Prix de Rome in 1914, a silver medal at the Salon des Artistes Français in 1927, and a gold one in 1929. The figures on the horizon, as well as the horse itself, suggest the influence of the Italian metaphysical painter, de Chirico.*

37. JEAN DUPAS, Woman in a Hat, *Gouache on paper dated 1926. Dupas won a gold medal for* White Pigeons *at the 1923 Salon des Artistes Français. His large painting* The Parakeets *was the focal point of Ruhlmann's* A Collector's Mansion *at the 1925 Paris exhibition.*

38. GEORGES LEPAPE, The Captive, *Gouache on paper, dated New York 1927. The pearls, real or fake, worn as a choker on a long strand were part of the fashionable uniform of the period.*

38

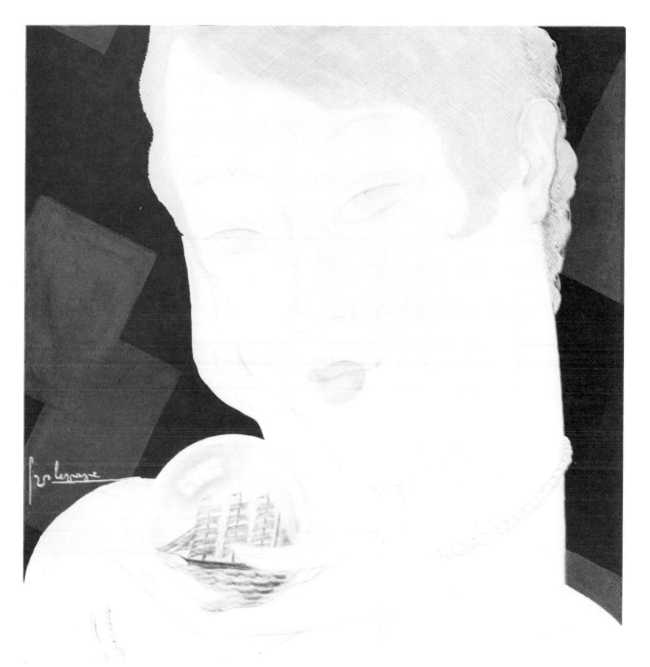

40

39. GEORGES LEPAPE, Design for
Vogue Cover, *Gouache on paper, 1930*.

40. GEORGES LEPAPE, The Dream,
Gouache on paper.

P. Dubaut

41

42

41. PIERRE DUBAUT, Polo at
Longchamps, *Water color on paper.*
*Pierre Dubaut made a reputation for
racing and polo subjects.*

42. PIERRE DUBAUT, Afternoon at the
Polo Ground, *Water color on paper.*
Reproduced in the periodical
l'Illustration, *2nd August 1930.*

13

43. LOSENZI, The Breast, *Gouache on paper.*
A liberated, bright young thing of the twenties. Note the fact that she is smoking with a cigarette holder and seems to relish it. Exhibited in Minneapolis Institute of Art, 1971.

44. JACQUELINE MARVAL, The Long Necklace, *Oil on canvas.*
A painter, lithographer and sculptor. She was the pupil of Flandrin and later became his wife. This is typical of her work.

45

45. VALENTINE GROS, Nijinsky in the Spectre de la Rose, *Water color on paper, dated 1912.*
Valentine Gros, wife of the Surrealist Jean Hugo, painted many portraits of the Russian dancer.

46. GEORGES LEPAPE, The Golden Sun, *Gouache on paper, dated 1914.*

46

48

47

47. ERTÈ, Fleurs de Mal, *Illustration for the book* The Orchid. *Gouache on paper, 1919.*
Romain de Tirtoff (Ertè) was born in St. Petersburg, came to Paris in 1912, began to design for Poiret in 1913. At first his work was presented under Poiret's name, but with the war, Ertè was able to work for himself. This costume and that in the next illustration were designed for the revue Gobette de Paris *at the Ba-ta-Clan theater.*

48. ERTÈ, Absinthe *for the* Fleurs du Mal, *Gouache on paper.*

49. ERTÈ, The Cloak, *for the* American Millionaires *New York. Gouache on paper.*
Ertè designed not only dresses, costumes for revues, operas and ballets, but also scenery for all kinds of theatrical productions. Later, he worked for films.

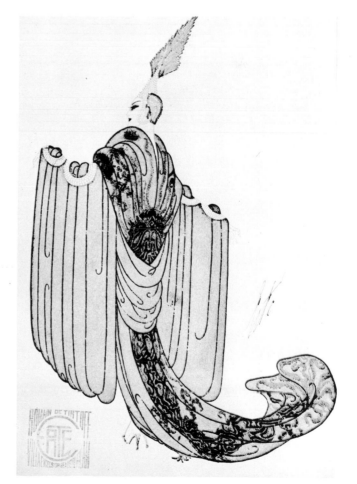

49

51

50. ERTÈ, Sadness, *Gouache on paper,
dated 1925.*
*Exhibited in Sonnakend Gallery, New
York, and Minneapolis Institute of
Art, 1971.*

51. PAUL COLIN, Nude, *Pastel on
paper.*
*Colin was the first to spot the potential
of the black American dancer,
Josephine Baker. He was the friend of
the jazz musicians and Negro dancers
who flocked to Paris in the twenties.
His striking posters helped to
popularize the jazz craze.*

52

52. JACQUES SOUBRIE, Ettore Bugatti,
Poster.
Bugatti cars became the symbol of
speed and modernity.

53. R. GERI, Bugatti, *Poster.*
Another advertisement for the famous
motor cars.

54

54. JENINE AGHION, Bilitis, *Gouache on paper.*
In advanced circles, hints of lesbianism were fashionable. One of those who enjoyed the notoriety brought by a somewhat ambiguous reputation was the writer and musical star Colette.

55. CHARLES GESMAR, The Black Diamond, *Gouache on paper.*
Gesmar was a Rumanian who died at only 28. He designed costumes and posters for the musical star, Mistinguet. Exhibited in Minneapolis Institute of Art, 1971.

55

le diamant noir

56. GUSTAV MIKLOS, Woman's Head,
Bronze with gold inlay.
The precocity of technique is typical of
the period as is the highly polished
surface. The face shows the influence
of African-Negro art.

2   S C U L P T U R E

Much the same influences were at work on the sculptors associated with the Art Deco style as shaped the work of the painters and illustrators. Here, too, we find the same tendency to keep a decent distance from the real avant-garde of the period, while nevertheless making use of certain of its discoveries—though usually it took some time for innovations to be absorbed. Yet there are also a number of factors which influenced sculpture alone. Some of these are aesthetic, others purely social, others still are a mixture of both.

      The Art Deco period saw a change in the way in which sculpture was used. During the nineteenth century, successful academic sculptors exhibited large works at the annual Salons, making reduced versions of the most successful for sale to the public. But they did not rely on sales of this kind. Buildings were nearly always lavishly decorated with sculpture, both inside and out; new public monuments were constantly being commissioned—many of them inspired by the rampant nationalism of the period; and there was a fashion for elaborate tombstones and funerary monuments. After the war, architecture became much plainer and more severe, tombs became less ostentatious, and, after the numerous commissions for war memorials had been allocated, public sculpture went out of fashion. As a result of this, interest turned to smaller and more intimate forms of sculpture.

      The man whose influence overshadowed that of all others on the rising generation of sculptors was of course Rodin. It was his impressionism, as much as the academicism of the immediate past, that the Modernist sculptors rejected, though many of them began by working in the same idiom. Brancusi is a notable example. Conservatives, too, had to come to terms with

Rodin's towering personality.

One of the means by which they sought an escape from Rodin's vision was by studying the art produced by ancient civilizations and by primitive cultures. It was not merely that the Cubists, abetted by the Surrealists, made African art fashionable, but that the period saw the real break-up of the confined European view of art history. Work which previously had been regarded as "curious," or at best as exotic, was now examined seriously for its own sake. It was the beginning of what André Malraux was later to dub the *musée imaginaire*, the process whereby all the products of man's aesthetic impulse were brought together and became at least intellectually, if not physically, available. The illustrations included in this book show numerous traces of the process I have described. For instance Jouve's bronze plaque of a panther (PLATE 69) demonstrates the influence of the Assyrian reliefs which had long been there for artists to see in the Louvre and the British Museum. The coati by Le Bourgeois (PLATE 81) shows the impact of Egyptian bronzes of the Late Period. These were very fashionable with the collectors of the twenties, and their compact forms, delicate stylization and smooth finish helped to flavor much of the animal sculpture of the time. On the other hand Franz Barwig's *Dancing Gazelle* (PLATE 82) has the look of Achamaenid work.

It is no accident that the examples I have just cited are depictions of animals. The sculptors of the nineteenth century had created a tradition of small-scale animal sculpture which was even better established that that of using animals as subject-matter for painting. These sculptors had even been provided with a special name—they were the so-called *animaliers*.

The most celebrated was Barye, but not far behind him in reputation came men such as Frémiet and Mène. The style that typified them was extremely naturalistic—it corresponded to the contemporary fashion for naturalism in painting.

One of the first *animaliers* to move away from doctrinaire naturalism was Rembrandt Bugatti. Strictly speaking, he cannot be labelled Art Deco as he committed suicide in 1916, when the style was still in its infancy. Nevertheless, he exercized an important influence over sculptors working in the twenties. The charm of his work (PLATES 57 to 66) lies in his ability to suggest qualities—stiltedness, litheness, ponderousness—without making all the details of appearances absolutely explicit. That is, what we are aware of in his work is a process of translation and transformation, rather than of imitation. The longer we look at any Bugatti sculpture, the more we come to realize that the marks which suggest the texture of fur and feather are as much a response to the method of making—scraping the clay model, pressing it with the thumb—as they are to the tactile suggestions conveyed by what was seen. Bugatti's work seems almost as lively, and indeed restless, as that of his predecessors, but the urge toward greater simplification, and toward a more conceptual view of form, was already making itself felt. This tendency was to culminate in the work of the greatest animal sculptor of the twenties, Francois Pompon (PLATE 79).

Pompon made his reputation late. He was already 67 when he scored his first great success in the Salon d'Automne of 1922. He had previously worked on monumental sculpture, and had studied under Rodin, as well as under more academic artists such as Mercié and Falguière. Pompon rebelled against the tradition of his predecessors in two respects. The form was now more stylized—the artist aimed to present not a momentary view of the subject, but a synthesis of observations made over a long period. Secondly, Pompon liked highly polished surfaces which caught the light and invited the caressing touch of a finger-tip. These shining surfaces emphasized the underlying geometry of the forms, and at the same time suggested that bronze could vie with more precious materials, such as ivory and hardstone. Other leading *animaliers* of the time—among them Guyot, Sandoz, Prost, Petersen and Le Bourgeois—move in much the same direction as Pompon, but are more reluctant to abandon the nineteenth century tradition of naturalism.

Sculpture which took the human figure, rather than the animal creation, as its subject matter, was subject to a variety of conflicting influences. One of these, of course, was the seduction of African art, already strongly felt by the pioneer Cubists before the First World War. The great popularizer of the "primitive" style for fashionable consumption was Gustave Miklos. A comparison between the female head by Miklos (PLATE 56), and a head by Modigliani (PLATE 88), will serve to illustrate his strengths and weaknesses. The Modigliani is more radical, but it is also much less sure of itself, and rougher. Miklos has reduced the subject to a series of forms which are the expression of a coherent decorative system. Both these heads ultimately derive from a well-known type of African mask, with oval eyes, a long thin nose, and a characteristic pinched mouth. But Miklos sees to it that black Africa is tamed and made fit for the Faubourg St. Honoré.

A much more powerful influence on the decorative sculpture of the epoch was traditional neo-classicism. However, it was a different kind of neo-classicism from that which had been practiced at the beginning of the nineteenth century by Canova and Thorwaldsen. The reason for this was again the dominating artistic personality of Rodin. The middle-of-the-road sculptors of the twenties were in reaction against Rodin, but they could never escape from him. They were engaged in a constant dialogue with his achievement.

The leaders of the return to classicism were Maillol and Bourdelle. Neither is particularly fashionable today, but one can at least do them the justice of noting the way in which they sought, not merely for a renewal of classical forms, but for a release of the pagan spirit. The lesser sculptors who followed in their wake—men such as Wlerick, Guino, Bernard, Janniot and Bouraine—produced work which is only now being reconsidered, after a period of almost total neglect. What one notices about it is its competence, and the absence of hypocritical prudery. The less ambitious neo-classical figures of the period—a good example is the stone figure by Janniot which appeared as part of Ruhlmann's exhibit at the 1925 exhibition (PLATE 98)—have some of the unpretentious charm of the decorative sculpture of the eighteenth century.

The neo-classicism of the interwar period only over-reached itself when it was seized with delusions of grandeur. There is not much to be said for the statues of muscular heroes and cloyingly perfect women which were made for the Trocadero buildings, designed to house the Paris 1937 exhibition.

In addition to making small sculptures of animals, the artists of the Art Deco period had another speciality— chryselephantine work on a small scale which originally meant the juxtaposition of ivory and gold. There was quite a large production of statuettes in which hand-carved ivory or imitation ivory is used in combination with gilded and patinated metal, and small pastes or semi-precious stone (PLATES 105 to 107).

The initial impulse for the production of work of this type seems to have been supplied by the Belgian government, who wanted to encourage artists to use the ivory which was then, at the end of the nineteenth century, coming out of their rich colony in the Congo. Sculptors were given free supplies of the material to experiment with, exhibitions were organized, and prizes awarded. Ivory was therefore often used in Art Nouveau sculpture. In the twenties the technique was revived, and small decorative figures were produced in Paris, Vienna and New York.

No one took these particularly seriously as works of art at the time at which they were made. They fulfilled much the same kind of function that figures in porcelain, *biscuit de Sèvres* and terracotta had performed in the elegant interiors of the eighteenth century. The main outlets were not art galleries but jeweller's shops and department stores, and they can be found advertized in contemporary department store catalogues. Estab-

90

lished sculptors made them—one who did so was Bouraine (PLATE 107), but there were specialists in this kind of work, the most gifted of whom was probably D. H. Chiparus (PLATES 105 and 106). Among the other signatures which appear on this kind of work are those of Frederick Preiss, Lorenzl, Colinet, Le Faguays, Bruno Zack, Godard and Philippe. Preiss was Chiparrus's chief rival in terms of quality.

Today these beautifully made statuettes have acquired enormous period charm, and are much sought after. They seem to encapsulate the atmosphere of Art Deco more successfully than work which was more ambitious and more seriously intended. In this respect, they are the three-dimensional equivalent of the fashion illustrations made by Georges Lepape.

57

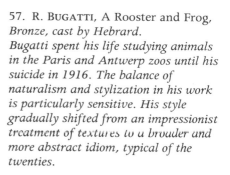

57. R. BUGATTI, A Rooster and Frog, *Bronze, cast by Hebrard.*
Bugatti spent his life studying animals in the Paris and Antwerp zoos until his suicide in 1916. The balance of naturalism and stylization in his work is particularly sensitive. His style gradually shifted from an impressionist treatment of textures to a broader and more abstract idiom, typical of the twenties.

58

59

58. REMBRANDT BUGATTI, The Secretary Bird, *Bronze, cast by Hebrard.*

59. R. BUGATTI, Buffalo, *Bronze, cast by Hebrard.*

60. R. BUGATTI, Ostrich, *Bronze, cast by Hebrard.*

60

61

62

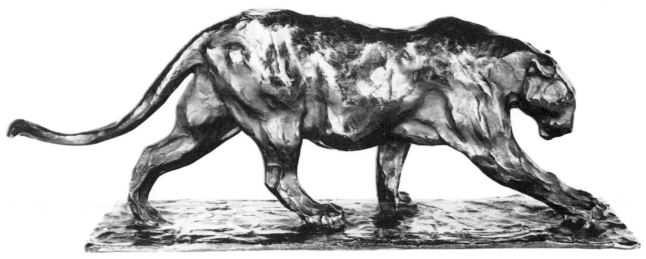

63

61. R. BUGATTI, Kangaroos, *Bronze, cast by Hebrard.*

62. R. BUGATTI, Snake, *Bronze, cast by Hebrard.*

63. R. BUGATTI, Walking panther, *Bronze, cast by Hebrard.*

64

64. R. BUGATTI, Gazelle Cannu,
Bronze, cast by Hebrard number 1.

65. R. BUGATTI, Two Does, *Bronze,
cast by Hebrard.*

66. R. BUGATTI, Walking elephant,
Bronze, cast by Hebrard.

65

66

67. EDOUARD-MARCEL SANDOZ, Cockatoo, *Bronze, cast by Valsuani Sandoz, born in Bâle, studied in Paris and exhibited at the Salons. His work has a degree of stylization, but is basically realistic.*

68. EDOUARD-MARCEL SANDOZ, Shark, *Bronze, cast by Valsuani.*

67

68

69

69. PAUL JOUVE, The Panther, *Bronze plaque.*
Bronzes by Jouve are rare. Note the Assyrian influence.

70

70. M. PROST, The Panther, *Bronze, cast by Susses Frères*
Prost was a follower of Jouve but does not have the same force and vitality.

71. REMBRANDT BUGATTI, Walking Jaguars, *Bronze, cast by Hebrard.*

72. GEORGES-LUCIEN GUYOT, The Panther, *Cast by Susses Frères.*
Guyot was another artist who sculpted and painted animals all his life. He exhibited at the Salon des Artistes Français, and later at the Salons des Independants and D'Automne.

71

72

73

73. GEORGES-LUCIEN GUYOT, Cat,
Bronze, cast by Susse Frères.

74. GEORGES HILBERT, The Bulldog,
*Bronze, cast after granite original.
Dated 1926 and numbered 1.*

75. L. SCHULZ, The Eagle, *Bronze,
cast by Valsuani.*

76. PAUL JOUVE, Lion with his kill
Bronze, cast by Alexis Rudier.

74

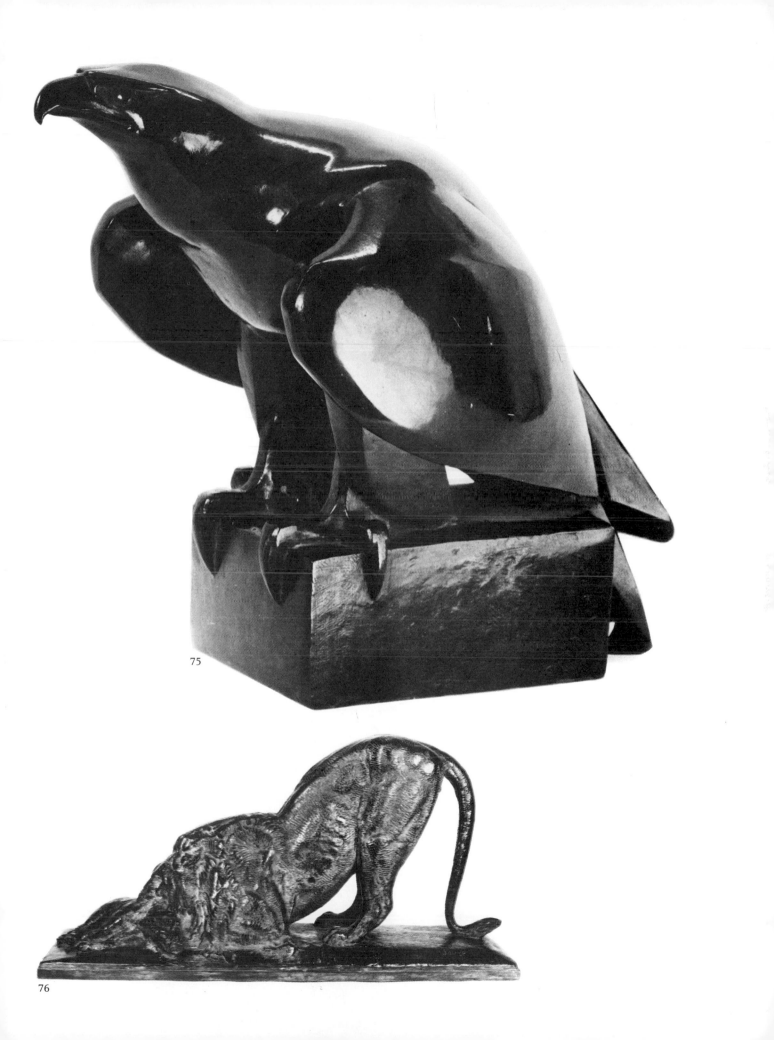

75

76

77

78

77. ARMAND PETERSEN, The Gazelle,
Bronze.
Born in Bâle, he exhibited at the Salon
D'Automne and the Tuileries.

78. EDOUARD-MARCEL SANDOZ,
Feneck, *Bronze, cast by Susses Frères.*

79. FRANCOIS POMPOM, The Deer,
Bronze.
The uneducated son of a provincial
cabinet maker, Pompom did not make
a real reputation until he was 67.
He studied with Rodin among others,
reacting against Rodin's romantic
realism. He started producing
simplified sculptures of animals with
highly polished surfaces, scoring his
first big success in 1922 at the Salon
D'Automne with a Polar Bear in
white marble.

79

80

81

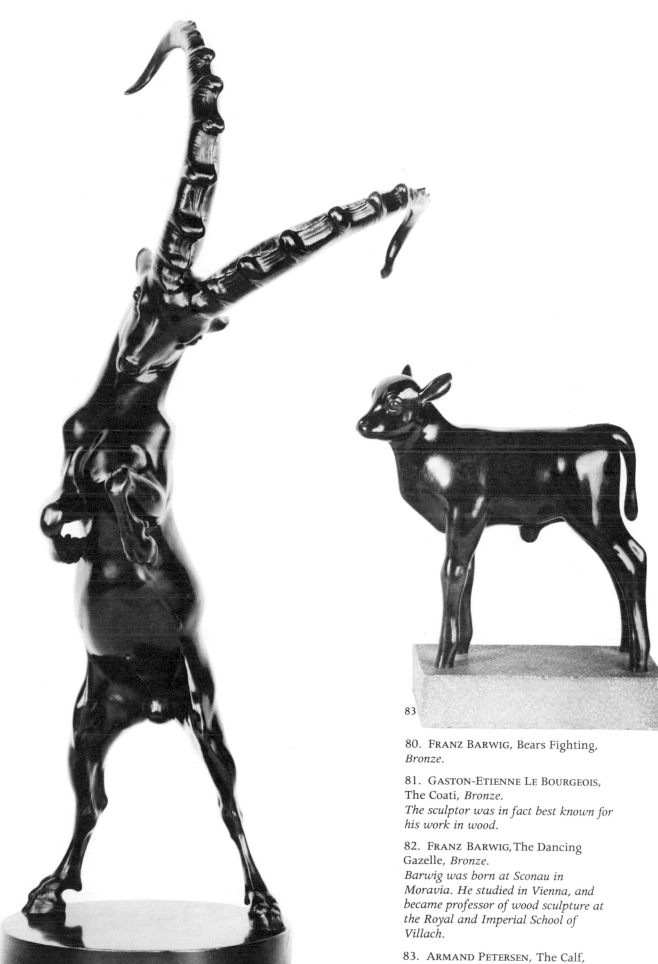

82

83

80. FRANZ BARWIG, Bears Fighting, *Bronze.*

81. GASTON-ETIENNE LE BOURGEOIS, The Coati, *Bronze.*
The sculptor was in fact best known for his work in wood.

82. FRANZ BARWIG, The Dancing Gazelle, *Bronze.*
Barwig was born at Sconau in Moravia. He studied in Vienna, and became professor of wood sculpture at the Royal and Imperial School of Villach.

83. ARMAND PETERSEN, The Calf, *Bronze.*

84. SIMONE MARIE, Two Hens, *Gilt bronze.*

85

85. GUSTAV MIKLOS, Singing Bird,
Bronze, 1929.
Miklos designed applied arts in Paris
after the war before turning to
sculpture. He had a one-man show in
1928 at the Gallerie of the periodical
La Renaissance. *He is now regarded as*
one of the most typical art deco
sculptors.

86. GUSTAV MIKLOS, Abstract figure,
Silver plaque, dated 1922.

87

87. AMADEO MODIGLIANI, Head of a
Woman, *Bronze, cast by Valsuani.
Modigliani wanted to be a sculptor but
was prevented from making many
pieces due to bad health and lack of
money. He took lessons from Brancusi,
showed at the 1912 Salon D'Automne
and ceased to make sculpture in 1915.
He preferred carving to modelling – the
bronzes were cast after his death under
the direction of his daughter.*

88. AMADEO MODIGLIANI, Head,
*Bronze, cast after a head in oak by
Valsuani. Note the strong African
influence.*

89. ROBERT WLERICK, Head of
Woman, *Bronze, cast by Alexis Rudier.
Wlerick's works are similar in feeling
to that of Charles Despiau, who came
from the same town, Mont-de-Marsan.
Rodin praised his contribution to the
1912 Salon.*

89

88

90

91

90. RICHARD GUINO, Leda, *Terracotta.*
Guino, already a trained sculptor,
worked under the direction of Renoir
from 1913 to 1918. The painter's sons
were later obliged by court to recognize
Guino's part in this collaboration.
After Renoir's death, he returned to his
personal work.

91. RICHARD GUINO, Adam and Eve,
Sevres biscuit.

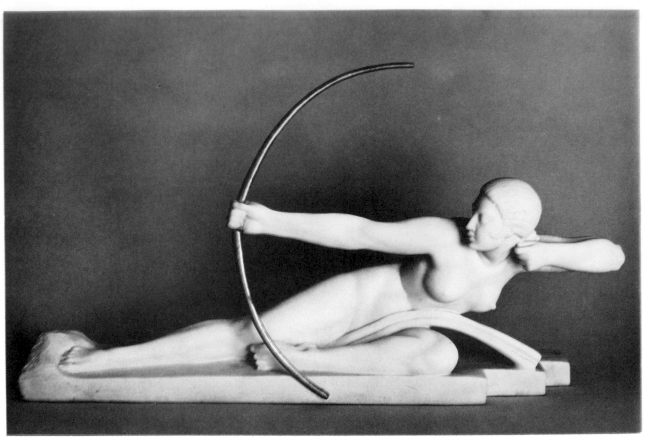

92

92. BOURAINE, Amazon, *Marble.*
Amazons by Bouraine are also found in
bronze and in parte-de-verre by
Argy-Rousseau.

93. CORMIER, Draped female figure,
Bronze, cast by Barbedienne. 1930.

94. RICHARD GUINO, The Offering,
Bronze, number 1.

93

94

95

96

97

98

95. JOSEF BERNARD, Female bust, *Gilt bronze, cast by Valsuani. 1920.*

96. JOSEF BERNARD, Dancers, *Bronze, cast by Alexis Rudier. 1926.*

97. JOSEF BERNARD, Girl Lifting her Hair, *Bronze, cast by Valsuani. Bernard worked all his life in Bologne. At first influenced by Rodin, he found a personal style in 1905. IIis work relates to that of Maillol and Bourdelle and was exhibited at Musée Rodin in 1972.*

98. ALFRED-AUGUSTE JANNIOT, Female Nude, *Stone. Formed part of a group of figures in front of Ruhlmann's stand at the 1925 Paris exhibition. Janniot is best known for the monumental frieze in stone made for the Musée des Colonies, which formed part of the 1931 exhibition at Vincennes.*

99

100

99. ANON. Cossak Dancer.
Illegibly signed piece which shows a strong Cubist influence. From the Bugatti collection.

100. PHILIPPE DEVRIEZ, Dancer,
Bronze with green patina.
Born in Poland, Devriez exhibited at the Salons des Artiste Français.

101

101. RAPHAEL SCHWARTZ, Female
Nudes, *Bronze, cast by Valsuani.
Born in Kiev, this artist showed at the
Salons Nationaux, D'Automne, and
Tuileries.*

102

102. MAURICE CHARPENTIER-MIO,
Dancers, *Bronze plaques.*
The large plaque shows Anna Pavlova
and Alexander Volinine in the ballet
Flocon de Neige, *given at the Theatre*
des Champs-Elysées in 1919. Both
dancers had previously come to Paris
with Diaghilev in 1909. The second
plaque is dated 1920, the third 1917.

103. R. PHILIPPE, Female Nude,
Bronze, with green patina.

103

104

104. PRINCE PAUL TROUBETSKOY, Portrait of a Seated Woman, *Bronze, cast by Valsuani.*
A Russian aristocrat who studied in Milan, Troubetskoy made portraits of fashionable people which had a great success in the United States as well as in Europe. His work is the sculptural equivalent of Boldini and De Lazlo.

105. D. H. CHIPARUS, Tamara, *Ivory, silver and gilt bronze.*
Chiparus is the best-known author of the Chryselephantine statuettes sold during the late twenties and early-thirties in big stores and jeweller's shops. The technique of juxtaposing ivory and precious metal goes back to antiquity. In the late 19th century, the Belgian Government started trying to encourage artists to use the ivory which came from their colonies in the Congo.

106. D. H. CHIPARUS, Dancers, *Ivory, patinated bronze and precious stones.*

105

106

107. BOURAINE, The Rearing Horse, *Ivory, silver and patinated bronze. Statuettes such as this were popular as Christmas or wedding presents. The purchaser could choose his own marble or onyx base.*

108. EDOUARD-MARCEL SANDOZ, Head of a panther, *Bronze, cast by Valsuani, marble base.*

107

108

109. EMILE-JACQUES RUHLMANN
Project for Ruhlmann's A Collector's
Mansion *in the 1925 exhibition*
He collaborated with many of the
leading Art Deco craftsmen, among
them Dunand, Decorchemont,
Mayodon and Legrain. There were
sculptures by Despiau, Pompom,
Bourdelle and Le Bourgeois and
pictures by Jean Dupas.

3   F U R N I T U R E

Although Art Nouveau did not come to an abrupt end in 1900, furniture underwent a remarkable transformation in France during the following decade. The work of the older generation of designers degenerated. Majorelle, Plumet, Bellery-Desfontaines, Gaillard and Tony and Pierre Selmersheim continued to produce pieces which had the curving lines and floral motifs of classic Art Nouveau design, but the carving became less fine and the shapes heavier and clumsier. Around 1904–5, Henri Rapin, Paul Follot, Lambert, Louis Jallot, Maurice Dufrêne and Fernand Nathan began to work in light-colored woods, using stylized decoration carved in low relief, and small inset panels of marquetry. The mainstream designers seemed bent on a return to Louis XVI classicism, with some concessions to the comfort of Louis-Philippe furniture. An exception to this was the work of Frantz Jourdain, who was later to be president of the Salon d'Automne. He created white-painted interiors which, though rather self-consciously rustic in feeling, anticipated the search for light, space and hygiene which was to preoccupy leading decorators of the twenties.

The early Art Deco style, which was triggered off by the arrival of the Ballets Russes in 1909, can also be dubbed the "boudoir style," because of its emphasis on rich detail and intimacy. The taste for anything oriental led to a fashion for cushions with long silk tassels, for textiles with mixed patterns and vivid colors, for low divans and day beds. The proportions of furniture began to change. Armchairs became longer and deeper, and stood on lower legs; dining-room chairs had small, rounded backs—more convenient when the diner was being served by the maid or butler; dining-room tables now had a single central pedestal, instead of four or six legs—this change, too, was also in part dictated by considerations of comfort. In the bedroom, beds were lower and built-in cupboards were being widely used for the first time. Sideboards (*bahuts*) and cabinets with a single door—types of furniture which had been popular in the eighteenth century—returned to favor.

As people began to live in smaller spaces, furniture tended to become smaller; and, even where large rooms were available, the tendency now was to put the emphasis on areas of unbroken space. After the first fashion for orientalia and pattern on pattern had subsided, the tendency was to harmonize colors and textures. Upholstery matched the carpet; the same kind of wood was used for panelling as had been employed to make the furniture. These carefully unified interiors were frequently and radically transformed, at least by those who aspired to be fashionable. The shortage of accommodation, even for the comparatively well off, meant that it was worthwhile to keep the same apartment, and to achieve the desired change of atmosphere, not by moving, but by total redecoration. And it is worth noting that the apartment now became the norm: most of the clients who could afford to pay for modern interiors had abandoned up-and-down houses for more easily managed quarters, all on one floor. In these apartments one space flowed into another, and a cohesive style was therefore easier to achieve. Most apartments were centrally heated, and this made for less formal arrangements of furniture.

The development of the Art Deco style brought with it a change, not only of forms, but of materials and finishes. Walnut and oak went out of favor, and the taste was now for more exotic woods, often with a decorative pattern or grain. Among the woods used were amboyna, amaranth, olivewood, sycamore, thuya, Cuban mahogany, Rio palissander, lemonwood, ebony and macassar ebony. These gave a strikingly wide color-gamut, ranging from the very pale to the very dark. It was the middle tones, on the whole, which became unfashionable. Some furniture was painted—chairs could be grey, gold or silver, with simple mouldings. A basket of stylized flowers would be used as a backrest. On case furniture, which was usually veneered, there was sometimes a restrained use of marquetry, usually in ivory, though Sue and Mare and Leleu experimented with mother-o'-pearl. Very fashionable cabinet-makers—Rousseau, Groult, Ruhlmann and Mère—made extensive use of shagreen. This treated fish skin, with its pale green color and intricate scale-pattern, became one of the hallmarks of the Art Deco style. Lacquer was also in high favor.

The real trend-setters were no longer individuals, but certain designers and decorating companies.

Poiret gave a powerful forward impulse to the "boudoir style" when he founded the firm of Martine in 1911. This began as a school for artistically inclined children but soon developed into a full-scale decorating company. Martine produced textiles, wallpaper, porcelain, pottery and hand-woven carpets, and the workshops decorated furniture designed by Pierre Fauconnet. It was therefore possible to find all the elements needed for a complete environment at the same source.

The most aristocratic, though not the most innovative, of the Deco designers was undoubtedly Ruhlmann. The furniture he produced was the equivalent of the superb work which had been done for the French court during the eighteenth century by cabinet-makers such as Reisener and Weisweiler. As a decorator, he was noted for his restrained and extremely individual color-schemes. His rivals liked the hot reds, mauves, greens and yellows of the Fauves; and the lavenders and pinks of Marie Laurencin. Ruhlmann was content with harmonies of black and gold, grey and silver, brown and white.

Once the Art Deco style had established itself, it began to be popularized for a wider and less affluent clientele. The great department stores opened workshops of their own to make furniture in small series which would nevertheless be cheaper than the commissioned pieces which came from independent designers. Furniture of this sort was still the product of artisans' hand labor. There was no direct link between factory and retailer, with many forms being dictated by the capacities and limitations of the machine and the assembly line. This only came about later on.

The first designers to form associations with the big department stores were veterans of Art Nouveau. Paul Follot, with his associate Laurent Mauclès, became director of "Pomone" at the Bon Marché in 1923; while Maurice Dufrêne founded "La Maîtrise" at the Galeries Lafayette. These two enterprises were soon rivalled by others.

At the same time, certain individualists flourished. One of these was Pierre Legrain, whose lack of training as a cabinet-maker meant that he could more easily conceive new forms, avoiding the trap of merely modernizing the traditional. In addition to designing tables and cabinets in lacquer, he was responsible for a series of seats inspired by African models; and for original, simple and elegant furniture in pale sycamore and chrome.

Marcel Coard, like Legrain, made unique pieces of furniture for Doucet and other collectors. He used sheets of parchment, shagreen, layers of tinted glass, mirror, and decoration in amethyst and mother-o'-pearl.

133

Equally original was the work of Eileen Gray. She had a great affection for lacquer; and the interest of her work is to be found in the unusual outlines and forms she employs, rather than in mere surface decoration.

As the decade progressed, furniture evolved. The whole feeling became heavier and more geometric. Legs became more solid; ornamentation tended to disappear and certainly became less flowery. Contemporary books on decoration talk of "hygiene" and "convenience" as prime essentials. The post-war servant shortage had begun to bite, and sparse, compact furniture with smooth surfaces exercized a distinct attraction for this reason alone.

1925 supplies a key date, because this was the year of the Paris *Exposition des Arts Decoratifs et Industriels Modernes*. The show gave Art Deco its name. Each decorator had a stand of his own—a reconstruction of a room or shop, and this enabled him to show, not merely objects, but a statement of decorative philosophy. Nevertheless, the objects themselves attracted considerable attention, and much of the furniture on display was bought by museums, notably by the Metropolitan Museum in New York.

With the 1925 exhibition, there came about a division of styles. While the decorators with basically traditional preoccupations, however inventive they were about details of form and decoration, continued on their appointed way, the architectural school, the true "modernists," at last began to make progress. For political reasons, Germany did not participate in the 1925 exhibition, and the work being done at the Bauhaus under Walter Gropius was still little known in France. Le Corbusier's pavilion, "*L'esprit Nouveau*," had little success, largely due to official obstruction, but it was a sign of the times.

In 1930, Le Corbusier and a number of other architects and designers such as Pierre Charear, Djo-Bourgeois, René Herbst, Francis Jourdain, Roger Mallet-Stevens, Eileen Gray and Jean Charles Moreux formed the *Union des Artistes Modernes*. They proclaimed that they were anti-past styles, anti-ornament, and in favor of the machine and the "beautiful in the useful." Advanced designers, such as those who attached themselves to the Union, no longer thought of furniture as something separable from the interior in which it was placed—it was, for them, an integral part of the way the architecture functioned. As far as France was concerned, Le Corbusier and his associates were the pioneers of "design" as we now know it. They made extensive use of steel, aluminum, glass and plain tough leathers: they were interested in stackable and transformable furniture. Comfort they admitted, but luxury they found otiose.

The formation of a new design-philosophy was accelerated by the Wall Street crash of 1929. Even in France, which escaped the worst consequences of the Depression, private patrons tended to draw in their horns financially. For men like Ruhlmann, Leleu and Dunand the important clients were now institutional ones: they continued to furnish banks, hotels, government buildings and ocean liners. Their work altered and coarsened as a result. Everything was now on a grand scale—what they were now called upon to design was massive and impersonal. Art Deco declined, not amidst the exaggeration and extravagance which have killed so many past styles, but into a kind of leaden nullity. It is doubly unfortunate that, simply because these later commissions were public ones, the worst aspects of Art Deco should have been so much more accessible than the best.

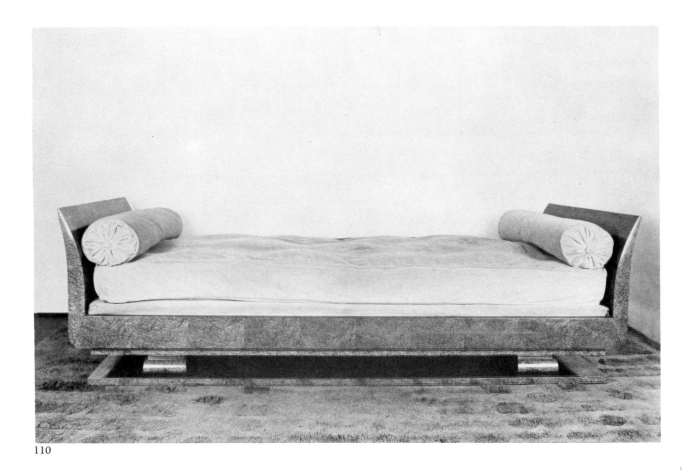

110

110. EMILE-JACQUES RUHLMANN, Bed, *Burr elm.*
Ruhlmann was the greatest cabinet-maker of the twenties. This bed goes back to French Empire models. Exhibited in Minneapolis Institute of Art.

111. EMILE-JACQUES RUHLMANN, Sofa, *Caucasian burr walnut, ivory, silver bronze feet.*
Unlike many of the 18th century cabinet-makers whom he rivalled, Ruhlmann paid particular attention to the finish of the furniture at the back and underneath.

111

112

112. EMILE-JACQUES RUHLMANN,
Dressing table, *Mahogany, ivory and
silver bronze.*
*This piece is typical of the work
Ruhlmann did in the early twenties.
Later his furniture became heavier and
more solid.*

113. EMILE-JACQUES RUHLMANN,
Dressing table, *Macassar ebony, ivory
and shagreen.*
*The carpet is also by Ruhlmann.
A dressing table of this model was
shown as part of Ruhlmann's
exhibition at the 1925 exhibition.*

114

114. EMILE-JACQUES RUHLMANN,
Circular dining table, *Macassar ebony
and chrome*. Made in the atelier B.

115. EMILE-JACQUES RUHLMANN, Roll
top writing desk, *Macassar ebony and
ivory*.

115

116

116. EMILE-JACQUES RUHLMANN, Pair of arm chairs, *Macassar, ebony and brocade.*
The upholstery here is influenced by African-Negro art and was especially designed to harmonize with the carpet seen in the photograph. Note the emphasis on luxurious comfort.

117. EMILE-JACQUES RUHLMANN, Two spoon-backed side chairs, *Macassar ebony with leather upholstery.*

118. EMILE-JACQUES RUHLMANN, Armchair, *Macassar ebony and silvered bronze.*
A chair of this model was shown in 1925. Screen in background by Dunand and carpet by Benedictus.

119. EMILE-JACQUES RUHLMANN, Dining chair, *Macassar ebony.*

117

118

119

120

121

120. EMILE-JACQUES RUHLMANN,
Armchair, *Macassar ebony and velvet.*

121. LOUIS SUE *and* ANDRE MARE,
Chair, *Light mahogany and tapestry.*
*Sue and Mare founded the Compagnie
Française in 1919. Many celebrated
artists worked for them. They
undertook commissions for Jean Patou,
Helena Rubenstein, Madeleine Vionnet,
and worked on the liners* Paris, Ile des
France *and* Normandie.

122. JULES EMILE LELEU, Pair of
chairs, *Walnut and chrome.*

123. PIERRE CHAREAU, Pair of
chairs, *Walnut, circa 1926.*
*Chareau belonged to a group of
architects who wanted to design
furniture which was beautiful because
of its forms rather than its
ornamentation.*

122

123

124

124. EMILE-JACQUES RUHLMANN, Low table, *Macassar ebony and ivory.*

125. EMILE-JACQUES RUHLMANN, Tripod table, *Macassar ebony and ivory.*
A table like this was also shown in 1925.

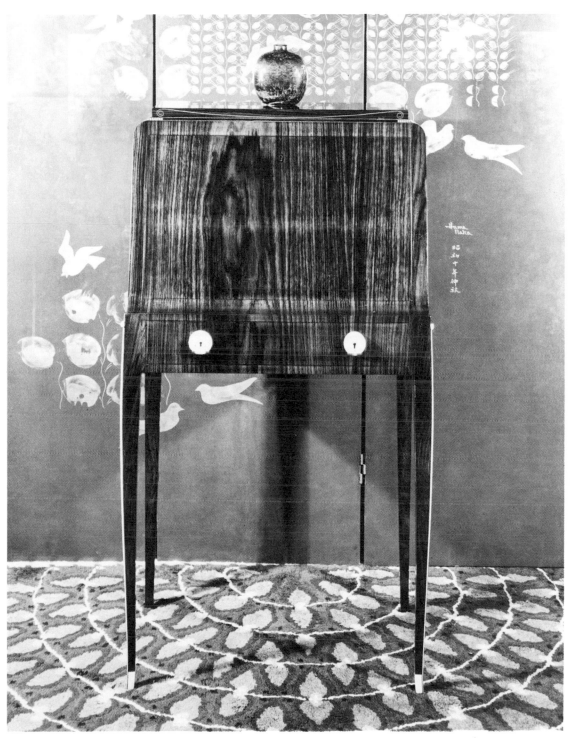

127

126. EMILE-JACQUES RUHLMANN,
Cabinet, *Walnut and ivory.*
A similar item was exhibited in 1925.
Ruhlmann made several pieces of this
type which were designed to be used in
traditional fashion between two
windows.

127. EMILE-JACQUES RUHLMANN,
Woman's desk, *Macassar ebony and*
ivory.

128

128. EMILE-JACQUES RUHLMANN,
Dining table, *Macassar ebony
shagreen, ivory and chrome.*
*The originality here is the support –
a variation on the theme of the pedestal
which means that all the diners can
sit in comfort.*

129. EMILE-JACQUES RUHLMANN,
Cabinet, *Amboyna and ivory.*
*A piece of furniture identical with this
was exhibited in 1905.*

130

130. EMILE-JACQUES RUHLMANN, Low
table, *Caucasian burr walnut.*
*Part of a suite – other items can be
seen in Plate 98 and V. The arched
foot suggests the influence of the
fashionable African stool.*

131. JULES EMILE LELEU, *Commode,
Walnut and mother-of-pearl.*

132. JULES EMILE LELEU, Cabinet,
Walnut and mother-of-pearl.
*Leleu's decorating company continues
today. In the twenties and thirties, it
produced furniture of very fine quality
– most of the pieces were adaptations
of traditional form.*

131

132

133. FOUJITA, Tabletop, *Marquetry – burr wood, ivory and ebony.*
This shows the artists' spectacles and pipes which often appear in his paintings.

134.

134. MARCEL COARD, Dining room table, *Oak, the top in black marbrite. From the collection of Paul Cocteau. Shows the influence of African art. Coard, who was trained as an architect, had a decorators shop in the Blvd. Hausmann and later in the Avenue Matignon. He made unique pieces for discerning collectors.*

135. ANDRE GROULT, Small table, *Lacquered wood, shagreen top, ivory finials to the legs, from the collection of Jacques Doucet.*
Groult's works are solid, comfortable and for the most part, traditional.

136. CATSU HAMANAKA, Lacquer table. *This Japanese artist worked in Paris.*

135

136

137

137. *Possibly by* MAURICE DUFRÈNE, **Chest of drawers**, *Amboyna and chrome.*

138. CLEMENT MÈRE, Armchair, *Macassar ebony, ivory, repoussée leather.*

Mère is best known for pieces showing intricate and complicated techniques – his decorative style features insects, petals and shells. In addition to furniture, he designed everything from carpets to jewellery. The carpet in this photograph is by Da Silva Bruhnes.

139

139. JEAN LURCAT, Carpet, *Produced by Myrbor.*
This firm was directed by the wife of a French senator, Marie Cuttoli, who asked many distinguished artists to work for her. Between 1939 and 1936, tapestries were woven after cartons by Rouault, Leger, Derain, Dufy, Segonzac, Miro, Picasso, Marcoussis and Lurçat.

140. IVAN DA SILVA BRUHNS, Carpet.
Bruhns' carpets were inspired by Moroccan, Mexican, and African-Negro models. They are signed in full, or with a monogram, the colors usually being either dark brown on beige, or white on black on dark brown.

141. Carpet.
A variant on the floral theme.

142. Carpet.
Another floral design, perhaps influenced by Derain or by Dufy textile patterns.

143. Carpet.
Many decorators designed floral carpets to harmonize with their interiors. Ruhlmann used spirals, scrolls and stem motifs in rhythmic abstract patterns, often based on the African-Negro textiles. The designer of this one seemed to have been influenced by the work of Cezanne.

140

141

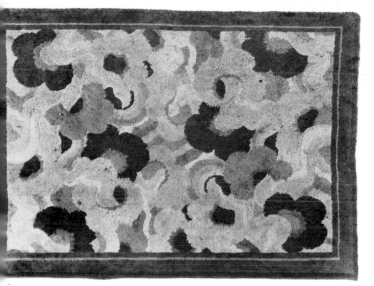

143

142

144. GEORGES LEPAPE, Cover for
Vogue. *Gouache, dated 1925.*

4 FASHION

Fashions in dress and fashions in interior decoration are, of course, closely linked, as we project our self-image through the clothes we wear even more than we do through the surroundings we choose for ourselves. At the beginning of the nineteenth century, for example, women wore neo-classical clothes to match their neo-classical furniture—high-waisted, pleated dresses made of thin muslins. At the end of the century women's clothes were both clumsy and elaborate, in step with the clumsy elaboration of many decors. The dress worn by the well-to-do women was so constricting, and often so cumbersome, that she had to be a person of leisure, as well as of means, to indulge in the folly of wearing it.

In 1903, a great innovator entered the fashion scene. Paul Poiret opened his first shop. He was a former employee of Jacques Doucet, and was therefore familiar with Doucet's perfect taste, then at its most *dix-huitième*. Poiret, however, was not in love with tradition of any kind. In due course he persuaded women to abandon their whalebone corsets, and to wear clothes which were easier and more fluid than any which had been seen since the days of Napoleon's Empire. Poiret introduced transparent colored stockings (which were considered shocking); he put tunics over tight skirts which reached to a point just above the ankle; he made a new coat-shape, with raglan sleeves and a billowing back; he told women to slash their skirts in order to reveal knee-high morocco boots.

It was Poiret who made oriental fashions chic. After the arrival of the Ballets Russes, he put his models into gold lamé turbans, and dressed them in eighteenth century Persian woven silks. He went so far as to experiment with tunics over gauze trousers, in order to get a "harem" look. This brought him plenty of notoriety, but did not catch on.

Poirét's line was essentially a vertical one, and the slimness he demanded was emphasized by the use of "difficult" Fauve colors. The full curves of the Belle Epoque were now no longer admired. Women had to transform themselves—to be beautiful, they must now be straight and tall, with slim hips and small busts. A step towards the new slim look was to get rid, not only of voluminous skirts, but also of layers of unnecessary underclothes. When the latter went, they went forever.

One reason for Poiret's impact was his flair for publicity. He wanted to control his clients' lives in every aspect, and he made his own scents, so that they should not only look like Poiret, but smell of Poiret, in addition to founding his his own decorating firm, Martine, whose mission was to see to it that their homes matched the clothes they bought from him.

The fashions of the immediately pre-war years did, however, have their irrational side. The hobble skirts of 1910–13 constricted movement to a ludicrous extent, and the wearer was forced to adopt a special tittuping walk to get about in them. It was the war which did away with the hobble-skirt, as with so much else. Women took an increasingly active part in the conflict, and many became accustomed to wearing a uniform—a far more practical and rational form of clothing than anything they had been used to in civilian life. Rationing made shorter skirts, not a statement of immorality, but a simple necessity.

The skirts of the twenties were not all short, as we now sometimes mistakenly suppose. Hemlines went up and down. For most of the decade they were at mid-calf. They reached their highest point—just below the knee—in 1926, and then began to fall again. Other aspects of fashionable costume were a good deal more constant. Pearls were worn, either in chokers or in long strings; hair was bobbed, shingled or Eton cropped, in order to accommodate the cloche hats which women wore pulled well down over the eyes. Waistlines dropped from the natural position until they rested on the hips (this imposed an even greater cult of slimness); coats often had large fur collars; stockings were transparent; shoes had straps and chunky heels. For evening wear beading and fringing were popular, and silver lamé was a material long in vogue. Pajamas became a kind of cult. They were worn, not only as night attire, but for "lounging." Formal evening dresses were somewhat longer than day dresses—the necklines were high and modest in front but plunged behind to show a bare back.

Twenties fashions looked their best on those who were young and slender. Older women wore them neverthe-less—the movement of taste was too powerful to be resisted.

The social upheaval caused by the war meant that much of the clientele, even at the best couturiers, was *nouveau riche*. The designer had increased opportunities to impose his own taste on the socially uncertain. At the same time, the couture itself became increasingly commercialized. Fashion was big business, and changes were encouraged through a skillful use of press publicity. The old, enclosed world which Worth and his peers had known had silently departed.

The most successful dress designers of the time were often women—a curious fact, if one reflects on it, as fashion itself was often rather unfeminine and occasionally androgynous. *La garconne,* the boy-woman, was a type of the period. Among these female designers were Coco Chanel (the most durable of them all), Madeleine Vionnet, Nicole Groult (Poiret's sister), Suzanne Talbot and the Callot sisters. Jeanne Lanvin specialized in sports clothes, as did the house of Rodier. New types of luggage were developed—high society had been seized with a mania for travel, and the weekend habit also meant many short journeys in the course of a year. Louis Vuitton made trunks for suits, guns, rods, fishing tackle and golf clubs; others would accommodate a typewriter, books and files. A specialized form of suitcase would accommodate thirty pairs of shoes, with a drawer for boots and three for stockings. The variety of specialized luggage available indicated the fact that the "new simplicity" was still a highly artificial concept. And Vuitton's creations, though made of relatively light materials and eminently practical were still, as a contemporary writer put it, "beautiful enough to decorate the relative bareness of palaces."

About 1928, fashion began to feel the first breath of a major change of direction. Dresses were no longer tubular, and the waist had returned to its normal place. Bias cutting was starting to come in; pleats and tucking played an increasingly important part. Hair began to be worn longer, rolled under in a page-boy look, or coiled in a bun on the nape of the neck. It was now topped with a small hat, tilted forward, with veiling over the eyes. Coats still had fur collars, but differently shaped, and made of fox fur.

There was a good deal of emphasis put, as the thirties came in, on glamorous cocktail and evening dresses. Satin was in favour—white or ivory, or in shades of peach or nile green. In the evening, women were now bare-shouldered as well as bare backed; their dresses were clinging, and often intricately draped in the manner of the ancient Greeks. Around 1938, the skirts of these evening dresses became very full, and elbow-length gloves were worn. At the same time, where day clothes were concerned, shoulders began to be accentuated with padding and swagger coats came in—these were later to be worn over trousers or short skirts during the war. Hats became much more dramatic—the most exaggerated creations (some associated with the designer Elsa Schiaparelli) were inspired by Surrealist painting.

During the thirties, the influence of Paris ceded to some extent, as far as the great mass of women were concerned, to that of the Hollywood stars, whose tastes and whims were widely publicized. It was Hollywood which created the fashion for platinum blonde hair. The magazines which dictated to women were now American-based—*Harper's Bazaar* and *Vogue* took the place of the *Gazette du Bon Ton* and *Fémina*. Nevertheless the Paris couture survived, and attracted a wider and more international public than ever before. The couturiers now presented their collections twice a year in older to attract orders from wholesale buyers, most of them from abroad. Elsa Schiaparelli, ever an innovator, started a ready-to-wear department as early as 1935. And by the end of the decade, when war broke out, the Paris fashion industry settled into much the pattern we know now.

145. GEORGES BARBIER, Madame Paul Poiret. *Gouache, dated 1913.*
Illustrates the vogue for Thousand and One Nights *orientalia, which had seized Paris since the arrival of the Ballet Russe in 1909. Note the aigrette in the hat.*

145.

147

146. GEORGES BARBIER, The strange
Bird, *Gouache*.
*Note the high waist and the fashion for
tunics during the immediate pre-war
period.*

147. GEORGES LEPAPE, The Print
Collectors, *Gouache*.
*High-waisted empire style dresses in
light or striped materials were also in
fashion just pre-1914.*

148.

149

148. GEORGES LEPAPE, Portrait of
Pauline Pieffer, *Gouache on paper.*
The sitter was Ernest Hemingway's
second wife and directed Paris Vogue.
Lepape was a regular contributor.

149. GEORGES LEPAPE, Fashion design,
Gouache.
In 1906, Poiret designed an evening
coat Confucius, *with a billowing back,*
which became the prototype for the
series of his creations and dominated
coat styles for years.

150

150. GEORGES LEPAPE, *Gouache.*
Combines two favorite themes of the
period – The Sultana in her harem,
and The Pierrot.

151. GEORGES LEPAPE, Balloons,
Gouache.
Suits for little boys in Europe were at
this time often based on sailor's
uniforms.

152. GEORGES LEPAPE, The Muff,
Gouache, dated 1913.
Illustrated in the Gazette du Bon Ton
1913, Issue 1.

153. GEORGES LEPAPE, Marcelle
Demay, *Gouache.*
*Lepape was the illustrator of an album
of Poiret's dress designs which was
published in 1911.*

154. GEORGES LEPAPE, Hat, *Gouache.*
*Hats were extravagant just after the
war, a reaction to the severity of
uniform.*

153

154

155

155. GEORGES LEPAPE, Shoes,
Gouache, dated 1924.
Shoes with long pointed toes were worn
with transparent pastel-colored
stockings. Another fashion launched
by Poiret which brought cries of
outrage.

156. GEORGES LEPAPE, The Kid,
Gouache, dated 1924.
Designed for another perfume
advertisement, this time reflecting the
craze for things youthful and
American.

157

157. GEORGES LEPAPE, Mam'zelle
Victoire, *Gouache, dated August 1914.*
Designed for the advertisement, Le
Nouveau parfum de Rosine:
"Mam'zelle Victoire." Rosine was
another business owned by Poiret and
named after his eldest daughter. War
had just broken out, and even perfumes
had to be patriotic.

158. GEORGES LEPAPE, Design for
catalogue cover. *Gouache, dated 1912.*
The exhibition was La Comèdie
Humaine *at the Galerie Georges Petit.*

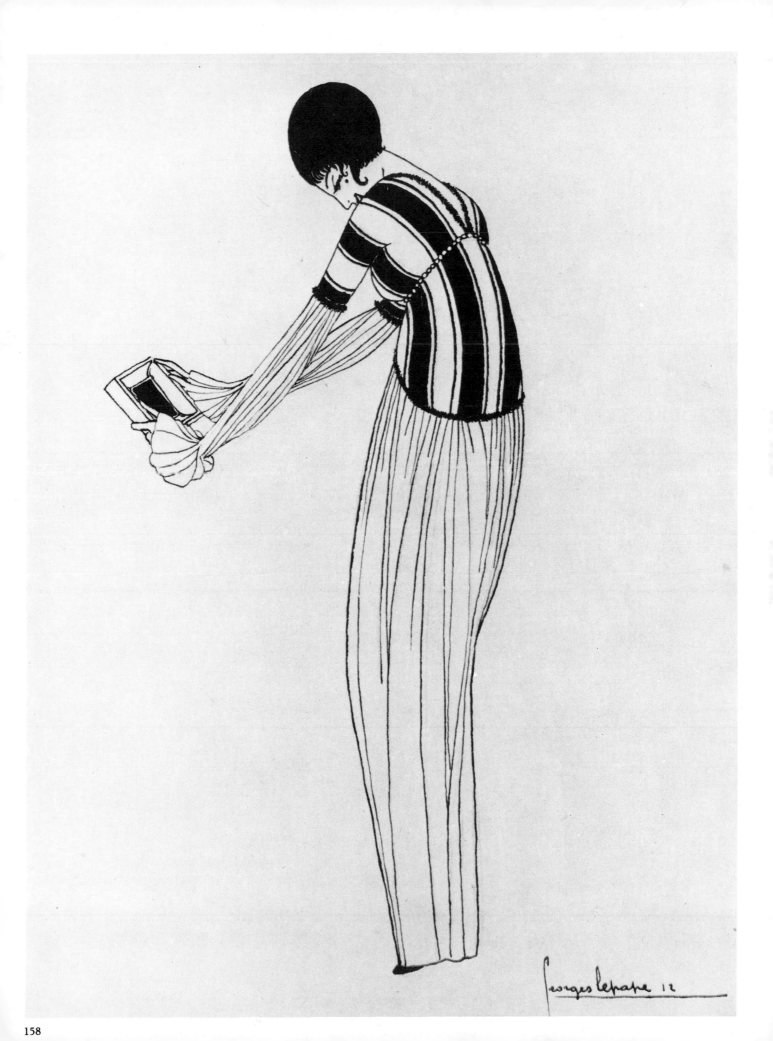

Georges Lepape 12

Pierre Brissaud 1920.

159

159. PIERRE BRISSAUD, Gossip, *Water colour, dated 1920.*
Reproduced in the Gazette du Bon Ton *1920. Vertical lines were emphasized by the use of pleats and panels of figured material.*

160. PIERRE BRISSAUD, Fashion design, *Water color, dated 1921.*
Hemlines dropped again around 1921–22 and skirts became fuller. Both these dresses have bateau necklines.

161. PIERRE BRISSAUD, Fashion design, *Water color, dated 1920.*
Just after the war, when hemlines went up and down, some designers compromised with the uneven "handkerchief" skirt, so this gave an untidy look when worn under a coat.

160

161

162

162. GEORGES LEPAPE, Fashion
design, *Gouache, dated 1923.*
In all the winter collections of 1923,
the cloche hat made its appearance,
necessitating bobbed hair. Note the
deco pattern of the fabric used for the
jacket.

163. ERTÈ, Fashion design: Fine
summer weather, *Gouache, dated 1916.*
It was the Gazette du Bon Ton *which*
began the habit of giving out narrative
captions fashionably.

163

164

164. ERTÈ, Fashion design, *Gouache,
dated 1916.*
*Marked on the back in French,
"Evening dress made with black and
white taffeta ribbons, the skirt is
formed of lace and ribbons."*

165. ERTÈ, Fashion design, *Gouache.
Ertè contributed his first cover for
Harper's Bazaar in January 1915.
He continued to design their covers in
1936. This drawing shows another
skirt with uneven points.*

165

166. GEORGES LEPAPE, The White
Dress, *Gouache, dated 1924.*
Intended for Vogue April 15, 1935, the
Paris exhibition of 1925 devoted two
large sections to fashion.

167. GEORGES LEPAPE, Fashion
design, *Gouache dated 1923.*
In all the winter collections of 1923,
the cloche hat made its appearance,
necessitating bobbed hair. Note the
deco pattern of the fabric used for
the jacket.

168A

168A. GEORGES LEPAPE, Evening dresses and coats, *Gouache, dated 1924.*

168B. GEORGES LEPAPE, Deauville. *Gouache, dated 1926.* *A good example of the "sporting" look of the middle twenties.*

169. PIERRE DUBAUT, A walk in the Bois de Boulogne. *Gouache, dated 1927.*
The man in the background is wearing plus fours or knickerbockers.

170. PIERRE BRISSAUD, Place Vendome. *Gouache, dated 1921.*
Note the full cut of the men's raincoats and the spats which all of them are wearing.

171. GEORGES LEPAPE, Cover for Vogue. *Dated 1928.*
Lepape was particularly good at depicting timeless elegance, despite Chanel's remark that "Haute couture creates beautiful things which become ugly whereas art creates ugly things which become beautiful."

169

170

173

174

172. GEORGES LEPAPE, Fashion
design. *Gouache, dated N.Y. 1926.*
Although the outline is simple, the
dress is made more interesting by the
subtle cut and the contrast of vertical
and horizontal lines.

173. GEORGES LEPAPE, Fashion
design, *Gouache.*
Demonstrates the romantic side of the
twenties – the dress is made of
gossamer, the new moon and the stars.

174. GEORGES LEPAPE, The Guitar.
Gouache, dated N.Y. 1927.

175. GEORGES LEPAPE, Cover for
Vogue. *Gouache, dated around 1925.*

175

176. GEORGES LEPAPE, Cover for
Vogue. *Gouache, dated 1930.*
*By 1930 hemlines had dropped right
down, waist lines were at their natural*
level, dresses moulded the figure, and
the cloche hat had disappeared in
favor of felt or fabric skull caps,
leaving the forehead exposed.

177. GEORGES LEPAPE, Cover for
Vogue. *Gouache, dated 1929.*
Maggy Rouff solved the hemline
problem by designing Spanish-inspired
ruffled dresses.

178. GEORGES LEPAPE, Cover for
Vogue. *Gouache, dated 1929.*
Nineteen twenty-nine was almost the
last year of very short hair. Soon it was
worn close to the head, waved over the
temples, then arranged in a bun or
rolled under on the nape of the neck.

179. GEORGES LEPAPE, Cover for
Vogue. *Gouache, dated 1929.*
This dress shows the trend which was to mark the twenties. With material cut
on the bias, soft draped necklines and
floating panels.

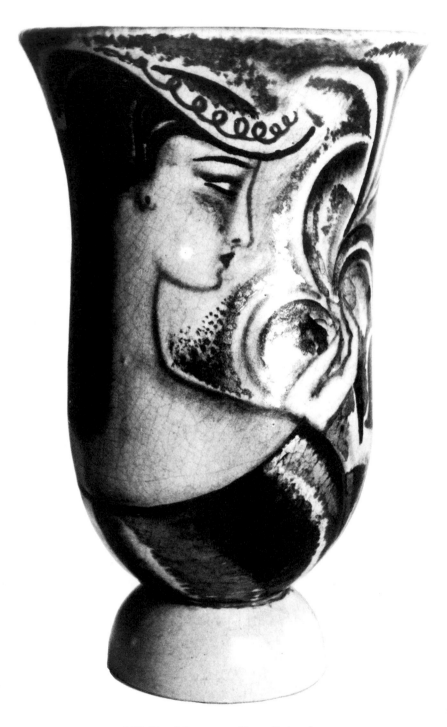

180. René Buthaud, Vase, *Painted faïence.*
Buthaud's faïence is hand-painted. Characteristic designs show elegantly dressed women or female nudes—the outlines are in brown or green.

5   CERAMICS

Fine stoneware had been one of the characteristic products of the Art Nouveau movement. With the renewed interest in the crafts so typical of the style, it was a matter of passion as well as of predilection. It summed up the dreams which were being dreamt at the turn of the century—stoneware created by the individual craftsman spoke of a return to simplicity; it accommodated the fantasies of Symbolism, incorporating, as it did, three of the four basic elements—earth, fire and water; it made a link with the renewal of interest in the Orient, and particularly the more transcendental kinds of Oriental religious philosophy.

The Art Deco ceramists, though equally capable and equally inquisitive technicians, were rather cooler in their approach. Instead of working secretly, savagely, bringing out the results only for rare exhibitions or for a few enlightened collectors who might buy, the twentieth century potters sought their clients through established retailers and regular Salons.

There was, however, the same eclectic search for knowledge—potters studied the wares of Persia, Turkey, Ancient Rome and Ancient Egypt. They were well-informed about current archaeological digs. But of all exotic civilizations, it was that of China which influenced them most, and Chinese monochrome glazes in particular that they were most inclined to imitate. This was in step with the collecting fashions of the time. It was the epoch when the interest of informed collectors switched from the late seventeenth and early eighteenth century polychrome wares which had fetched high prices in the Duveen era, to the Sung monochromes which had always been greatly valued by the Chinese themselves. The disturbed political condition of China meant that increasing quantities of these and other "Chinese taste" ceramics were becoming available in the West.

The precursor of the experiments made during the twenties with monochrome stonewares was Ernest Chaplet, whose thick-walled stonewares covered with rich *flambé* enamels are among the outstanding *tours de force* of the Art Nouveau period. But now it was Emile Decoeur whose work seemed to sum up the new spirit of objectivity. Decoeur was, among other things, an extremely objective judge of his own production. He broke anything which did not reach his own high standards. But he also had a wonderfully precise knowledge of how to achieve exactly the effects he wanted. His vases are classically simple in shape, and some pieces have slight ornamentation, either in relief or painted in enamels. But mostly they are monochromes, in shades of peach, green or dark brown, and also in black, sometimes with a black rim and interior to offset the pale color.

Another potter who took T'ang and Sung porcelains as his models—after first following Korean and Japanese examples—was Emile Lenoble. In his work, the enamels are granular and matt; Decoeur's, on the other hand, are shiny and smooth. Lenoble used black, beige, old rose, turquoise and green.

Among the leading potters of the period, in addition to Lenoble and Decoeur, were Felix Massoul, Fernand Rumèbe, Henri Simmen, Jean Besnard, Seraphine Soubdinine and Georges Serrié. Each has his own particular individuality. Massoul scores with his colors. Like Lenoble, he used turquoise, but his was the brilliant turquoise of the ancient Egyptians—he rediscovered the secret of this. He used modern oxides to evolve a characteristic deep green; and was also able to produce a fine *sang-de-boeuf* glaze, and one in a mixture of turquoise and white, fatty enough to resemble dripped colored candlewax.

Fernand Rumèbe was also one of those who was inspired by the Far East, but his stoneware resembles Chinese case glass, in which the colored outer layer is carved away in order to reveal the lighter opaque ground beneath.

Henri Simmen was of Flemish origin, and this perhaps accounts for the fact that his work is different in feeling from that produced by the other Art Deco ceramists working in the same field. His speciality was salt-glaze—the speckled effect which results when salt is thrown into the flames of a wood-kiln during firing. His characteristic ornamentation is in black and dark brown, with touches of gold. He made, in addition to his salt-glaze, pieces with thick celadon-green or off-white enamels, ornamented with abstract motifs in low relief. Rarely, he used a brilliant scarlet matte enamel. His Japanese wife, Madame O'Kin Simmen, sculpted ebony and ivory lids and stoppers for the vases.

Jean Besnard was the son of the painter Albert Besnard. What he made was a deliberately primitive stoneware, inspired by peasant pottery of the Mediterranean and of Savoie.

Quite different from what Besnard produced is the work of Seraphine Soubdinine, a Russian emigré who decided to become a sculptor on meeting Rodin. He then saw the fine collection of Far Eastern ceramics in the Metropolitan Museum, New York, and became involved with making stoneware, which he used as material for his sculptures. His brown glazes make use of contrasts of matte and gloss. His signature is two heads of seraphs.

Another potter who used dark brown glazes was Georges Serrié. Before the First World War, Serrié studied ceramics at Sèvres. During the war, he was taken prisoner, escaped from Germany, and was sent to Saigon. There he taught in local art schools, and began a fascination, which proved lasting, with Chinese and Khmer art. On his return to France, he built a wood-kiln at Sèvres, where he prepared his clay himself, and used it to make unique pieces of stoneware decorated with chevrons, stylized animals, etc. He had a successful exhibition at Rouard's; and this inspired a number of sculptors to ask him to produce their work in stoneware—they included Dejean, Gimond, Niclausse and Contesse. The color and "hammered" finish of these pieces makes them resemble bronze.

Perhaps more typical than stoneware of the ceramics produced in the Art Deco style are the pieces in painted faïence. The best-known name is that of René Buthaud, whom many regard as the Art Deco ceramist *par excellence*. The success of his work depends not so much on the quality of the glazes, as on the delicacy and freshness of his painting. On typical examples, the faces and figures of women are outlined in dark brown or black, and then washed with color—the style is distinctly reminiscent of painters such as Dupas, Pougheon and Lepape.

Another interesting faïencier was André Methey, whose importance is twofold. He himself was a dedicated experimentalist with glazes, and a charming painter, whose stylized flowers and leaves and naïvely drawn figures are admirably suited to the forms he chose. He employed thick, rich enamels, in turquoise, green, white, blue, grey and pink, heightened with crackled gold. In addition to producing his own work, he offered his pots as a canvas to his artist friends, among whom were many of the leading Fauve masters.

Methey was not the only potter to collaborate with artists in this way. The Catalan Llorens Artigas worked with Dufy, Miró and Picasso. Zadkine and de Chirico worked at the

National Manufacture at Sèvres; while Chagall, Gleizes and Vlaminck decorated vases and tiles.

The best-known specialist tile-maker of the period was Jean Mayodon, whose tiles were chosen for the *Normandie*. He was also a potter of some distinction. In this respect, his work resembles that of Methey, but is lighter in weight and not perhaps of the same quality. His green, orange and red enamelled vases and plates are decorated with mythological figures, gods, deer, centaurs and long-haired nymphs.

Buthaud's work in particular is now very much sought after by collectors, but there are minor makers of painted ceramics whose work has hitherto been somewhat neglected, and whose production is well worth attention. These include Claude Lévy, Mathurin Meheut, Cazaux and Charles Catteau.

During the twenties, the big stores began to narrow the gap between the ceramic industry and the artist potter, just as they attempted to do in the realm of furniture and decoration. Maurice Dufrêne designed tableware for *La Maîtrise* at Galeries Lafayette; the Printemps sold tableware of modern design under the trade name "Primavera," while "Longwy" was the name used for the brilliantly colored enamelled faïence sold by *Pomone* at the Bon Marché. Suzanne Lalique, Jean Luce and Edouard Sandoz all received design-commissions from the firm of Haviland. Sue et Mare (*Compagnie des Artistes Français*) made off-white services in the same style as their furniture, rounded, with a stylized leaf decoration. Georges Rouard, a shop in the Avenue de l'Opera, stocked ceramics decorated by Hermann Paul, Marcel Goupy, Drésa and Lucien Bonvallet.

The prestigious National Manufacture of Sèvres provides a special case—a mixture of work done by individuals, under the umbrella provided by the factory, and of work done in series. The direction of the enterprise had been taken over in 1920 by Lechavallier-Chevignard, and a new workshop for producing artistic faïence and porcelain was set up under Maurice Gensoli, who himself produced excellent pieces with smooth, deep grey, dark green and black glazes. Among the characteristic Art Deco products of Sèvres are semi-transparent chandeliers and wall appliqués in pierced and moulded porcelain, and sculpture in biscuit (unglazed porcelain) by Max Blondat, Charpentier-Mio and Jacques Nam. Striking vases were also produced—they were decorated by painters such as Brunelleschi, O. D. V. Guillonnet, Robert Bonfils and the ubiquitous Jean Dupas.

181. RENÉ BUTHAUD, Two vases,
Faïence.
*The left-hand vase is decorated in low
relief, and the design is emphasized by
the way the glaze has gathered along
the edges of the outlines.*

182

183

184

182. RENÉ BUTHAUD, Vase, *Painted faïence.*
Buthaud started as a painter and engraver, and turned to decorating ceramics after the war.

183. RENÉ BUTHAUD, Three vases, *Painted faïence.*
The vase on the right has a design inspired by a Persian miniature. The first serious collectors of Persian

manuscripts—these became available on the European market after the 1908 Revolution—included Jacques Doucet and Paul Poiret.

184. RENÉ BUTHAUD, Three vases, *Painted faïence.*
The woman on the middle vase can be compared to the women who appear in contemporary paintings by Matisse.

185

186

185. ANDRÉ METHEY, Two bowls,
Glazed pottery.
*Methey decorated many pieces himself,
in the style of the Fauve artists. He
signed with an M in a circle before
about 1909, and later with an A.M.
in a circle, with an impressed trefoil.*

186. ANDRÉ METHEY, Adam and Eve,
*Glazed pottery dish. Exhibited in
Musée de Sévres, 1970.*
*Methey was a self-taught potter, who
collaborated with many of the leading
artists of the time. At the 1907 Salon
D'Automne he showed ceramics
painted by Renoir, Bonnard, Durand,
Vlaminck and van Dongen, among
others.*

187. HENRI SIMMEN, Three vases,
Stoneware.
*Simmen, a Fleming, studied ceramics
in China and Japan. His salt glazes
usually have black and brown designs
picked out in gold. His wife, Madame
O'Kin, made ivory covers for many
other vases.*

188

189

190

188. JEAN MAYODON, *Faïence.*
At first sight Mayodon's work could be confused with Methey's, but is lighter in weight. The figures are thinly painted in green, orange, black and gold.

189. SÈVRES, Group of porcelains.
The designs used at Sèvres became less dependent on the past after 1900. Le Chavallier-Chevignard took over the direction in 1920, and these vases are typical of what was produced in the art deco style.

190. MAURICE VLAMINCK Vase
Pottery
Ceramics painted by Vlaminck are rare.

191. MAURICE GENSOLI, Bowl in Sèvres porcelain. *Dated 1925. Created by Ruhlmann.*

191

192

192. RAOUL DUFY *and* LLORENS
ARTIGAS, *Faïence.*
*The vase on the right is dated 11th
Oct, '26. Vase on the left exhibited
in Musée de Sévres, 1970. Dufy
collaborated with the Catalan
ceramist Artigas between 1922 and
1930 and again in 1937 and 1939.
Artigas also worked with Marquet,
Miró, and Braque.*

193. MAURICE GENSOLI, Porcelain.
*Gensoli made stoneware, porcelain and
pottery at Sèvres, where he was for
many years head of the decorating
department.*

194. MAURICE GENSOLI, Porcelain.
*Gensoli's glazes are simple and usually
monochrome.*

193

194

195

196

195. FERNAND RUMÈBE, Stoneware. *Rumèbe worked at first with Emile Decoeur. Ceramics by him are rare, as he never produced on a commercial scale. Note the Japanese influence. Exhibited in Munich at the Olympic Games, 1972.*

196. FERNAND RUMÈBE, Stoneware dish.

197

198

199

197. EMILE DECOEUR, Stoneware.

198. EMILE DECOEUR, Stoneware.

199. EMILE DECOEUR, Stoneware.
From 1939 to 1942, Decoeur designed forms for the Manufacture Nationale at Sèvres, who named him artistic advisor in 1942. Decoeur not only had complete technical control, but also a highly developed sense of the balance of color and form.

200. (OVERLEAF)
EMILE DECOEUR, Stoneware.
The greatest ceramist of the 1920s, Decoeur is famous for vases and bowls of pure outline and simple form, with monochrome glazes in yellow, blue, pink, green and white. His work is close to classic Chinese ceramics.

201

202

203

204

201. EMILE DECOEUR, Stoneware.

202. EMILE LENOBLE, Stoneware.
Lenoble was the grandson of Ernest Chaplet, a famous ceramist of the 1900 period. The technique used in these vases is that of scraping away the thick brown or honey colored slip to reveal the stoneware ground.

203. EMILE LENOBLE, Stoneware.
Around 1910–1912, Lenoble painted his stoneware with stylized flowers as seen here.

204. EMILE LENOBLE, Stoneware.

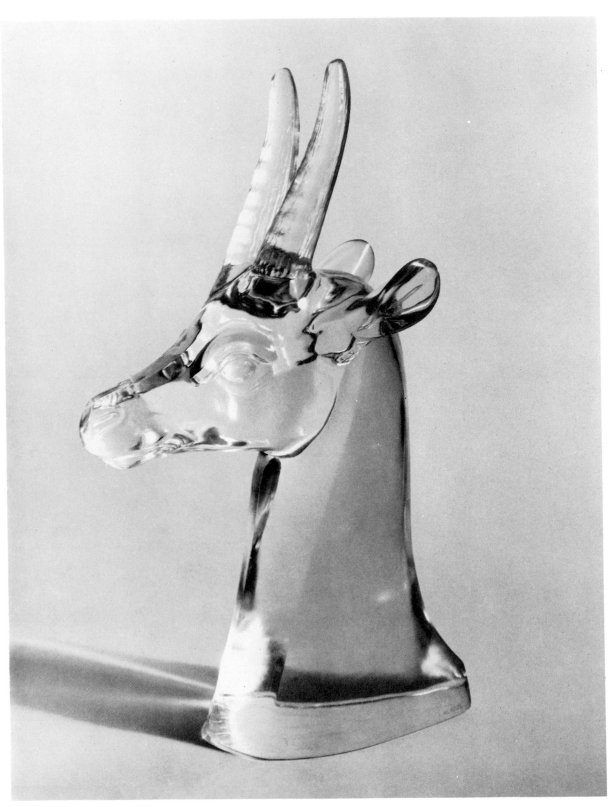

205. René Lalique, Crystal.
Made in one piece.

6   GLASS

Art Deco glass can be divided into a number of categories: first there is *pâte-de-verre*, *pâte-de-cristal* and *pâte-d'émail*—the leading maker of these is Decorchemont; secondly there is the blown and sculpted glass now usually associated with the name of Maurice Marinot; thirdly there is moulded glass—the most typical types were made by René Lalique; fourth and lastly there are the glass table-services made for the big stores, and other glass made by semi-industrial processes.

Pâte-de-verre is a term which may need explanation. Essentially, it is an opaque matter which results from firing crushed crystal and oxides in a mould at a temperature of 900 degrees. It is, however, often confused with the cameo-cut colored glass made by Emile Gallé, Daum and other members of the School of Nancy during the 1890's. *Pâte-de-verre* was made in the Art Nouveau period—Henri Cros used it to try and recreate the polychrome sculptures of the ancients. But its full development as an artistic medium had to await the arrival on the scene of the hand-prepared and fired work of François-Emile Decorchemont.

Decorchemont began his career as a ceramist and painter. Around 1900 he began experiments with *pâte-d'émail*. This is so fine that it resembles eggshell, and so fragile that little has survived. Decorchemont then started making heavier, more solid vases and dishes, with stylized geometric motifs in low relief. The deep colors, combined with qualities of translucence rather than transparency, made these pieces resemble hardstone rather than glass. Such pieces fitted the mood of massive luxury which many of the best Art Deco designers and decorators tried to create. Decorchemont's work can be placed on a par with that of Decoeur, Dunand and Ruhlmann. It was chiefly marketed through the firm of Rouard, but the long hours of hand-labor, and the technical processes used, made it commercially impractical.

G. Argy-Rousseau and Alméric Walter also produced *pâte-de-verre,* but in more industrial fashion. Their vases, small sculpture lights and wall-lights were made in moulds, in relatively large quantities for each model. Another maker was Jean Cros, son of the pioneer Henri Cros. He made panels resembling those produced by his father, but the detail is not so well-defined and the colors are rather acid.

Maurice Marinot, perhaps the greatest of all Art Deco glassmakers, is a craftsman whose work is even more sought after by collectors than that of Decorchemont. It is, unfortunately, extremely rare, as Marinot's merits were recognized by his contemporaries, and much of what he produced has disappeared into museums. Other examples were destroyed in the 1939–45 war. Marinot began his career as a painter—one of the Fauves—and started to paint goblets and vases at the glassworks which belonged to his friends Eugène and Gabriel Viard, at Bar-sur-Seine. He depicted stylized flowers and neo-classical figures in fresh, clear colors. He held an exhibition at the premises of the bronze-founder, Hébrard, and attracted a number of collectors, among them artists such as André Mare and Paul Véra.

In the twenties, Marinot's style changed radically. He abandoned enamels, and began to slash his crystal forms with deep acid-cut grooves, or to manipulate the material while it was still hot, treating the piece as if it were a sculpture. He took his inspiration from natural forms—ferns, frost-patterns, the veins of leaves—and tried to translate his observation of these into terms of the clouds of air bubbles or the fragments of metallic oxide which he trapped within the thick walls of his vases. Marinot's work seems like a magical collaboration between man and nature.

If Marinot and Decorchemont are the most creative glassmakers of their time, René Lalique is the one whose name has become a household word. "Household" in every sense, as he designed glass for the home, for everyday use, and not merely for collectors. Lalique was trained as a painter and goldsmith, and during the Art Nouveau period he produced some of the most sumptuous and imaginative jewels ever made—the most representative collection of his work in this medium is now in the Gulbenkian Museum in Lisbon. In the years immediately before the war he started experimenting with blown glass, and in 1908 he received a commission from the perfume-manufacturer François Coty for a series of bottles—the first time that perfume had been marketed in a distinctive packaging. After the war, he began to design moulded glass, to be made in power presses. The

220

presses and moulds were supplemented by the use of the *cire perdue* technique, employed for statuettes, elaborate stoppers, and some particularly large pieces.

Lalique's moulded glass was at first grey, but this color gave way to a milky blue. Other pieces were made in brighter blue, in orange, green and brown, and in clear crystal decorated with shiny black enamel. Among Lalique's typical products are vases, bowls, chandeliers, clock-cases, lamps and radiator mascots. The pieces are decorated with birds, leaves, deer, and figures of sirens in low relief or modelled in the round. Lalique's wares were immensely popular as wedding or anniversary gifts, and there were few prosperous households of the twenties and thirties that did not possess a piece.

With Lalique, we move into the region of industrial or semi-industrial production. One minor department of this was enamelled glass, produced by Auguste Heilegenstein, Marcel Goupy, Jean Luce, André Ballet, Georges Chevalier and André Deverin among others. The enamels they used were in shades of acid green, "Lanvin" (cornflower) blue, yellow, white, sugary pink, and orangy called "tango." Paul Poiret's pupils in the Martine workshops painted bottles with flowers, in which he marketed his perfumes.

Among the glass-making companies who produced original designs the most important were Daum, Schneider and Le Verre Français. Antonin Daum, together with his brother Auguste, had been one of the leading names in Art Nouveau glass. The firm now made two kinds of glass. One group used material which was smoked, clear, or grey, with bubbled or acid-cut decoration. A few rare pieces resemble Marinot. The other part of Daum's production was colored glass in shades of orange, dark green and blue, sometimes with inclusions of gold foil, and often with metal mounts by Marjorelle and Brandt. Schneider, still much undervalued, made bowls, vases and goblets on slender stems in opaque orange, mauve, acid green and yellow glass, with contrasting light and dark colors. Le Verre Français is also too little appreciated at the moment—their geometric and stylized animal designs, particularly those by Charder, are most decorative. Like Daum, they made lamps as well as vases. In these, the shiny mottled glass is acid cut to show the body color, and sometimes a piece of twisted glass is used as an inclusion in the foot, in place of an engraved signature.

Finally, there were the pieces sold, not under the trade-names of manufacturers, but under those of the big stores. Jean Luce, Suzanne Lalique and Maurice Dufrêne all executed commissions of this kind, and their work is often characteristic of the epoch.

206

207

206. FRANÇOISE DECORCHEMONT,
Pâte-de-verre.
The snake often appears as a motif in Art Deco, though no longer as the symbol of evil which the symbolists made it.

207. FRANÇOISE DECORCHEMONT,
Pâte-de-verre.

Decorchemont started as a painter, then turned to stoneware. In 1903 he began making bowls in eggshell thin enamel paste, but few have survived.

By 1925 he was making thick, heavy pâte-de-verre pieces, which resemble hard stones.

208

208. GABRIEL ARGY-ROUSSEAU
Pâte-de-verre
The Egyptian style was in vogue after the discovery of Tutankhamen's tomb in 1922.

209. (OVERLEAF)
RENÉ LALIQUE
Perfume bottles were a characteristic part of Lalique's production—he was first encouraged to make them by a commission from Coty.

210

211

213

212

210. GABRIEL ARGY-ROUSSEAU
Pâte-de-verre.
*In Argy-Rousseau's work the bodies
are usually thin and light in weight;
a few rare pieces are enamelled and
gilded on a crystal body. He was fond
of mauve, and pink topaz and rust.*

211. GABRIEL ARGY-ROUSSEAU
Pâte-de-verre.

212. GABRIEL ARGY-ROUSSEAU
Pâte-de-cristal
After a sculpture by Bouraine.

213. GABRIEL ARGY-ROUSSEAU
Pâte-de-verre.

215

214. FRANÇOIS-EMILE DECORCHEMONT,
Pâte-de-verre.
*Masks, animals and fish by this artist
are rare.*

215. ALMÉRIC WALTER, *Pâte-de-verre.*
*Walter's later work in acid-drop colors
has the creamy look of soapstone.*

214

216

216, 217. ALMÉRIC WALTER.
*Walter worked for Daum at Nancy
before setting up his own workshop in
1919. He collaborated with the
sculptors Henri Bergé, Bouraine,
Descomps, and Jules Chéret. The
reclining figure below was sculpted
by Joe Descomps.*

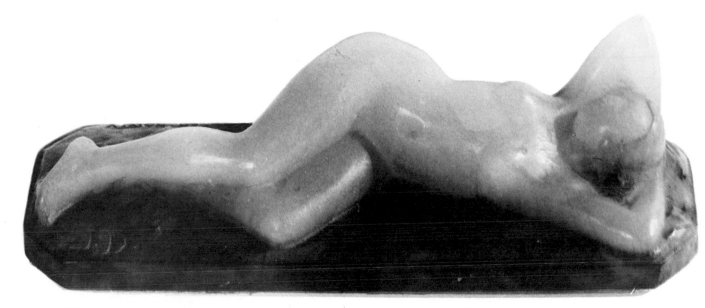

217

218

218. ALMÉRIC WALTER, Lamp,
Pâte-de-verre and onyx base.
Walter designed lights and wall
appliques in a yellow, green, and white
pâte-de-verre. They have often lost
their original mounts, unlike this
example.

219. DAUM, *Acid cut glass.*
The Daum brothers also formed part of
the School of Nancy. Antonin, the
surviving brother, made vases like this
in the 19th century, plus some rare
pieces which resemble Marinot.

219

220

221

222

220. DAUM, *Acid cut glass.*
Lamps like this by Daum are now unusual, though they must have been made in large series.

221. MAURICE MARINOT, Crystal.
Marinot wrote: "I think that a beautiful piece of glass should keep as much as possible the aspect of breath that creates it, and that its form should be a moment in the life of the glass fixed by the cooling."

222. MARINOT, Crystal.
Maurice Marinot began as a Fauve painter, then made enamelled glass from 1911–1922, and finally began to manipulate the glass itself. The imprisoned air bubbles are an especially typical effect.

223. MAURICE MARINOT, Two Vases, *Crystal.*
By the greatest glassmaker of the time. Marinot said: "To be a glass maker is to blow the transparent matter close to the blinding kilns; it is done with the breath of the lips and the tools of the glass makers' art; it means working in baking heat and smoke, with eyes full of tears and blackened and burnt hands."

223

224

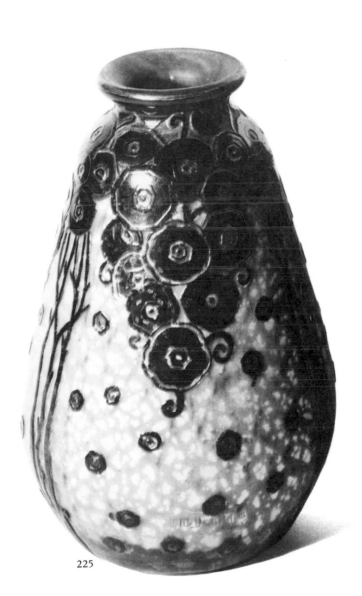

225

224. ANDRÉ THURET, Crystal.
Thuret began making glass in 1924.
Working single-handed at the factory
of Alforville, near Paris; his forms are
rounded and softened compared to
Marinot's.

225. MULLER, Glass.
The Muller brothers formed part of the
School of Nancy centered around
Emile Gallè during the 1920's. These
vases are in "cameo technique."
Small pieces of metal foil have been
placed in the glass to give a richer
effect.

226

227

226. Henri-Edouard Navarre,
Crystal.
A sculptor and medal-maker before turning to glass, Navarre's work is similar in feeling to that of Thuret. He made a few rare masks whose features are cut with acid.

227. Gabriel Argy-Rousseau,
Pâte de verre.

228. Marcel Goupy, *Enamelled glass. Goupy was the artistic director of Rouard in the Ave. de L'Opera who sold work by Navarre, Thuret and Decorchemont. He himself, designed enamelled glass and porcelain tableware.*

228

229. RENÉ LALIQUE, *Crystal.*
Parts of a large service.

230. RENÉ LALIQUE, *Moulded glass.*
Lalique glass varies in quality. In the early pieces, one finds nymphs, animals and grimacing masks in low relief or sculptured, as here, in the round.

230

231

231. RENÉ LALIQUE, Moulded glass.
*The left-hand vase has mounts in
forged iron by Brandt, an unusual
combination; while the jug on the right
is an early piece in greyish glass.
Dedicated to Pozzi by Lalique.*

232. *also* 240. RENÉ LALIQUE,
Moulded glass figure.

233. RENÉ LALIQUE, Moulded
opalescent glass.
*This is the most commonly imitated
type—imitators included Etling, Ezan,
and Hunebelle.*

232

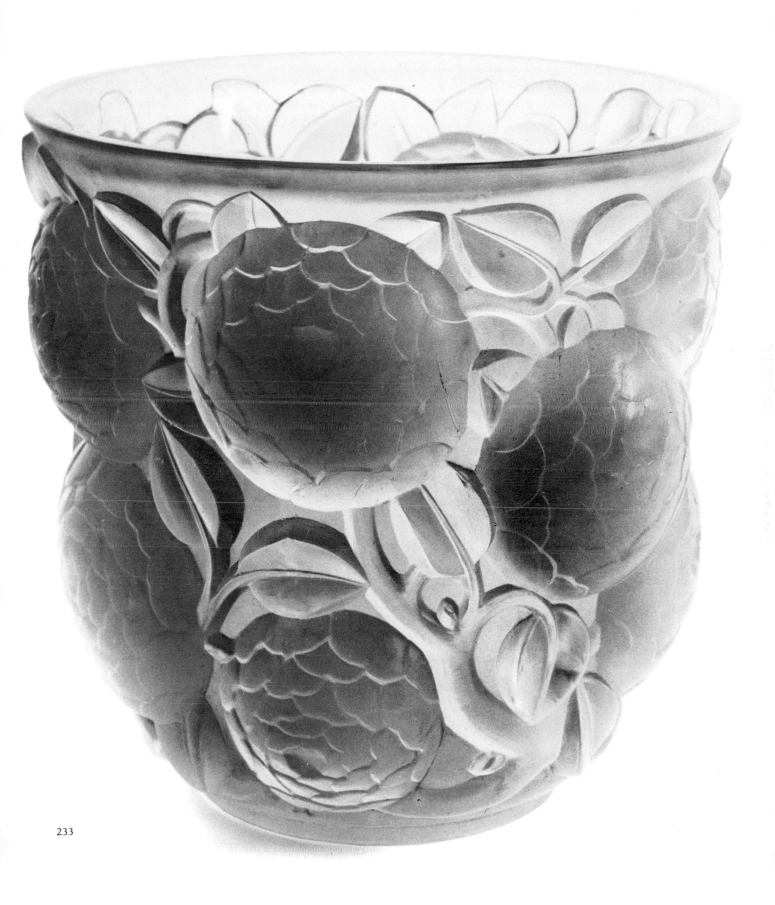

233

235

234. RENÉ LALIQUE, Moulded glass. *Around 1925 Lalique made some striking glass with the decoration in shiny black glass against a clear or white ground.*

235. RENÉ LALIQUE, Moulded glass figure.

236. RENÉ LALIQUE, Moulded glass. *The left-hand model is called "Petrarque."*

236

237

237. RENÉ LALIQUE
A good example of the attention paid to the detail on the ornaments. Vases like this often have a pale blue ground.

238. JEAN SALA, *Pâte-de-crystal.*
Jean Sala came from a family of Catalan glassmakers of Italian origin. They settled in France about 1906, and made a collection of fish for the Monaco aquarium. Jean Sala's work, which he made single-handed, is like ancient Roman glass.

239. RENÉ LALIQUE, Lamp, *Glass and bronze.*
The motif is intaglio. Lights by Lalique of this type are rare.

238

239

240. JEAN DUNAND, *Black lacquer panel.*
Dunand was the leading lacquerer of the 1920s. The model is wearing jewellery by the artist.

7   L A C Q U E R

Lacquer is one of the most characteristic materials of the Art Deco period. The technique of lacquering had fallen into virtual disuse in the West since the eighteenth century. In the reigns of Louis XV and Louis XVI, the great *ébenistes* had not only made use of coromandel lacquer panels imported from the Orient, but had actually perfected lacquering techniques of their own.

The rediscovery, in Paris, of the secrets of the lacquerer's craft was due to the Japanese artist Sugawara, who came to Paris at the age of 18. Unfortunately, we know little about his life and work. We do know, however, that Eileen Gray, an Irishwoman who had learned lacquer-restoring when she was in London studying at the Slade School of Art, met Sugawara after her move to Paris in 1907. She later collaborated with him over a number of years when she worked in the rue Visconti producing unique pieces of furniture. Later still, she opened a shop in order to sell furniture, carpets and lighting fixtures designed by herself and produced in small series, though this was never a great commercial success.

Eileen Gray's work is today a matter of some controversy. At heart, she was an architect before everything else, and she does not agree that her decorative work in the twenties should be classified as Art Deco, but insists that she was always, and from the beginning, a modernist. There is, however, a decorative side to her production during the teens and twenties. A superb lacquer screen, formerly in the collection of Jacques Doucet, and dating from 1913, has a figurative design on one side, and a completely abstract one on the other. This indicates the dichotomy then to be found in what she was producing.

Sugawara was also the teacher of Jean Dunand, whose meeting with him in 1912 completely altered his life. Dunand, already well-known as a metalworker, started to lacquer his vases in order to heighten the patina and surface decoration. After the war, he opened his own workshops, employing up to a hundred people, including a number of Indo-Chinese artisans, to make furniture, decorative panels and ornaments.

The range of Dunand's themes and techniques is quite remarkable. The black, tawny, brown, red and gold lacquer was painted, carved, "plucked" or sprinkled with fragments of eggshell. The surface could be highly polished or granular, flat or in low relief. The lacquer Dunand uses is thick, layer was applied upon layer, and the designs he used were almost as varied as his techniques. Some panels have abstract designs, the precursors of the "op" art and "hard edge" painting of the sixties; others show anecdotal scenes, realistic portraits and whimsical animals—it is probable that these last were drawn by the Polish artist Jean Lambert-Rucki, who collaborated with Dunand for a number of years. Dunand lacquered furniture made by Pierre Legrain, Jean Gouden, L. Ott, Eugène Printz, Ruhlmann, and by Ruhlmann's nephew Portneuve, who took over the firm after Ruhlmann died in 1933. He also lacquered sculpture by Miklos and Lambert-Rucki.

Dunand's work, being so laborious to produce, was necessarily expensive, but his firm survived the Depression. In 1931, he and his oldest son Bernard, who today restores lacquer, decorated part of the liner *Atlantique*; and in 1935 he contributed to the interior of the *Normandie*. The decorations in this ship were subsidized by the French government, in order to encourage the luxury trades. Dunand's work was technically ingenious. Large lacquer panels in low relief were divided up into smaller panels bordered with copper, to resist possible cracking due to the movement of the ship. The great door between the smoking-room and the saloon represented *The Hunt;* in the smoking-room itself was a fishing-scene in Egypto-Assyrian style, and a group of wild horses galloping.

We meet Sugawara once again in connection with another Japanese artist, Katsu Hamanaka, whom he initiated into the techniques of lacquering. Hamanaka worked with furniture designers such as André Domin, J. Adnet, Maurice Dufrêne, E. Y. Ruhlmann and Jules Leleu. His lacquer panels in brilliant gold and brown are finer in texture than those of Dunand. His figure paintings show muscular giants, and remind one both of the work of his compatriot Foujita, and of the designs favored by the ceramist Mayodon during the thirties.

Mention should also be made of Marcel Wolfers, son of Philippe Wolfers, the Belgian Art Nouveau goldsmith and jeweller. Marcel Wolfers met Dunand during the war, when they were helping to lacquer aeroplane components. During his career, he has been sculptor, ceramist, and lacquerer as well. He applied lacquer to his bronze and wood sculptures, made precious boxes, vases and bracelets, and also made unique pieces of lacquer in gold *wakasa nuri*, in deep red and in tortoiseshell, ornamented with ivory, mother-o'-pearl and lapis. Some bowls by Wolfers are made of lacquer only, without a wooden support, which have particularly attracted the interest of Japanese and Occidental collectors.

Jacques Nam worked, during the war, at the same factory as Dunand and Wolfers. He was above all a painter of animals, who used lacquer as a base for his work, and he often bought ready-made panels to paint or engrave, or used a synthetic lacquer, which lacks the depth and resonance of the true material, which requires up to twenty layers, each layer being hardened (in a damp room), filed down and polished, each layer in turn being "ripened" in the sun.

Nam's animals are more formalized than those of Paul Jouve, who used panels lacquered by Dunand. And Nam painted not only wild beasts but domestic cats, for which he had a passion.

A third *animalier* who painted on lacquer was André Margat, who exhibited his coromandel lacquer panels in Ruhlmann's shop from 1928 onwards, later specializing in large panels for public buildings.

A lacquerer working in quite a different style from those who have so far been mentioned was Paul-Louis Mergier, who combined a career as an aeronautical engineer with that of a metalworker and painter. He made furniture and large decorative panels. In the latter, stylized floral ornamentation and monumental figures in lacquer are combined with applied repoussé copper, a combination which gives an unusual contrast of sleek sophistication and the hand-crafted look. A specimen of his best work can be seen in the Musée des Arts Decoratifs in Paris—a manuscript cabinet made for Doucet, in green morocco, with ivory feet and the circular corners and central mount made in Japanese taste, using eggshell and mother-o'-pearl. The interior is lined with parchment. This cabinet is typical of the best Art Deco, combining refined simplicity with unusual and expensive materials.

Another craftsman represented in the Doucet collection was Edouard Degaine, two of whose small lacquer panels are to be found on a cabinet made for the collector by

Pierre Legrain. Legrain also designed a scarlet lacquer filing cabinet for Doucet, made in collaboration with Jean Dunand, plus a series of seats in brown and black lacquer inspired by African Negro models—some of these belonged to Madame Tachard, the *modiste* and friend of Doucet.

Besides Legrain, furniture makers who used lacquer included Paul Montegnac, Leon Jallot, Robert Mallett-Stevens, Jules Leleu, Sue et Mare and Rose Adler. Rose Adler often followed designs by Marcel Coard, whom she knew through Doucet.

Most lacquer, and particularly that of Dunand, Wolfers and Eileen Gray, was inspired by Japanese models, but there was also, in the twenties, a vogue for Chinoiseries. At the big store, the Printemps, Louis Sognot and Marcel Guillemard provided a Chinese-style Tea Room and a Chinese Salon. In more serious vein, Lahalle and Levard specialized in coromandel lacquer decorated with oriental landscapes—a Chinese rather than Japanese mode; and the great individualist among furniture designers, Marcel Coard, also interested himself in coromandel-style lacquer.

One of the curiosities of Art Deco is the work done in lacquer by A-A Rateau, better known for his bronze furniture. Rateau decorated Jeanne Lanvin's bathroom with lacquer with a pattern of deer and foliage in deep relief. For his own house, he made panels in yellow lacquer painted with birds, butterflies and leaves; and also a suite of furniture with a light layer of silver lacquer on a gesso ground.

241. JEAN DUNAND, *Black lacquer.*
*These doors came from a large cabinet
exhibited by Ruhlmann at the 1925
exhibition. The psychedelic dog and
hedgehog were drawn by Jean
Lambert-Rucki, a Pole who closely
collaborated with Dunand over many
years and helped to direct his
workshops.*

243

242. JEAN DUNAND, *Lacquer panel. Formerly in the collection of the artist's son.*

243. JEAN DUNAND, *Black lacquer and eggshell box.*

244. JEAN DUNAND, *Vases and a tray. Lacquer.*

245. (OVERLEAF) JEAN DUNAND, *Gold and black lacquer panel. A pair of panels which were studies for the decoration of the liner* Atlantique. *Although Dunand used the Japanese technique of lacquer, it is rare to find a Far Eastern-inspired composition, as in this panel.*

244

245

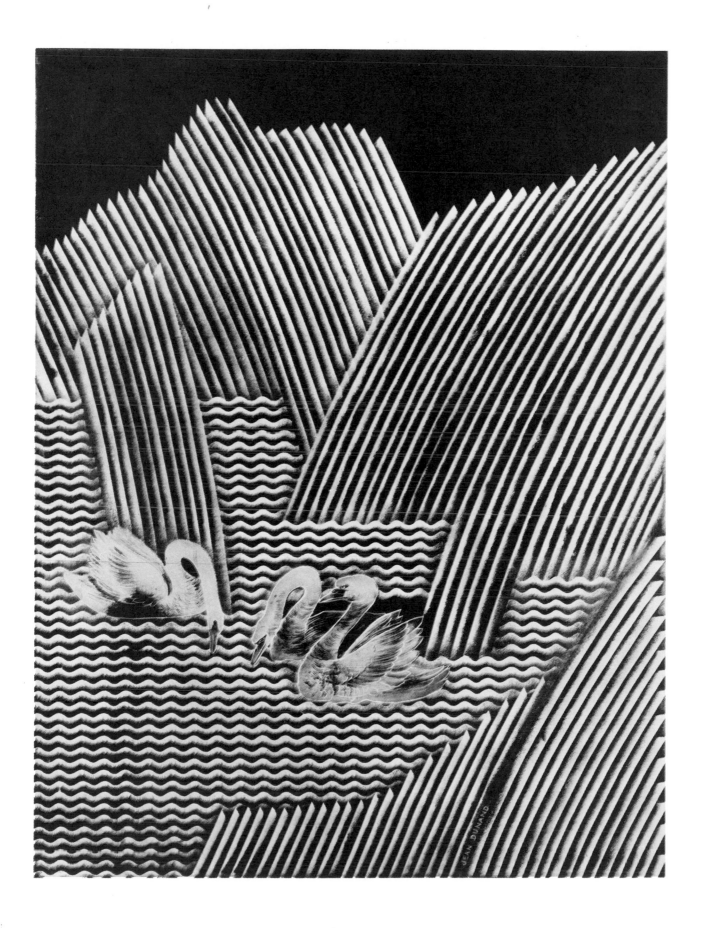

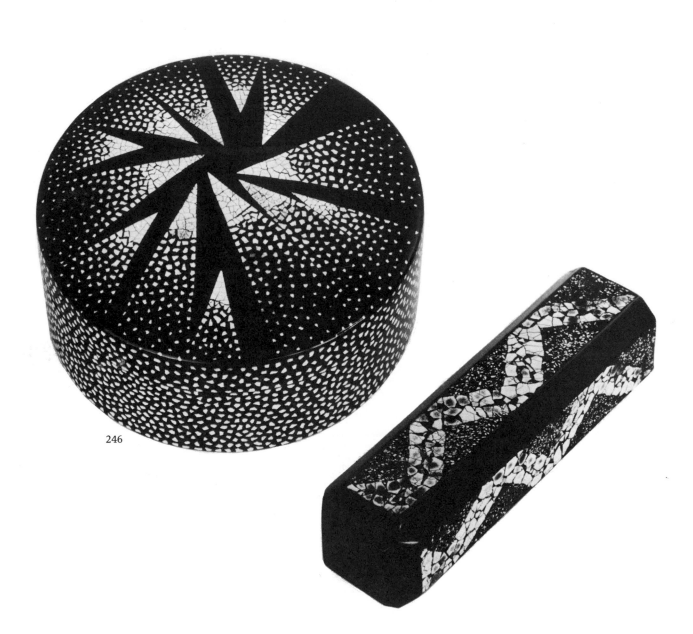

246

246. JEAN DUNAND, *Covered box and umbrella handle.*
Black lacquer and eggshell. This decoration with tiny fragments of eggshell is typical of Dunand.

247. JEAN DUNAND, *Lacquer screen. Another example of animals drawn by Lambert-Rucki.*

248. (OVERLEAF)
KATSU HAMANAKA, Rising Sun, *Gold lacquer.*
The sun burst motif recurs in Art Deco, woodcuts, posters, clothes, enamel boxes, etc.

247

249

249. JACQUES NAM, *Lacquer panels in the coromandel technique.*

250. JACQUES NAM, *Lacquer panels in the coromandel technique, with gold lacquer panels. Nam painted and engraved directly onto the already prepared gold metal panels.*

250

A. MARGAT 1932

252

251. ANDRÉ MARGAT, *Lacquer. Dated 1932.*
Margat exhibited his work from 1928 onwards in Ruhlmann's boutique. Much of it was bought by French or foreign museums. He also made huge lacquer panels for official buildings— these can, unfortunately, rarely be seen by the public.

252. JACQUES NAM, *Lacquer.*
Nam lived surrounded by his cats. He illustrated an album called Les Chats *with a text by Colette. He also made cat sculptures in bronze and Sévres porcelain. Nam often depicted wild as well as domestic cats and won a silver medal from the French society for the protection of animals.*

253. (OVERLEAF) KATSKU HAMANAKA, Two bulls, *Screen in brown lacquer on gold.*
The reverse is painted with birds and foliage. Signed in Japanese and French. Hamanaka began working in Paris in 1924, making shagreen furniture. He turned to making lacquer after meeting his compatriot, Sugawara, who had such a decisive influence on Jean Dunand's own career and who was working with Eileen Grey.

251

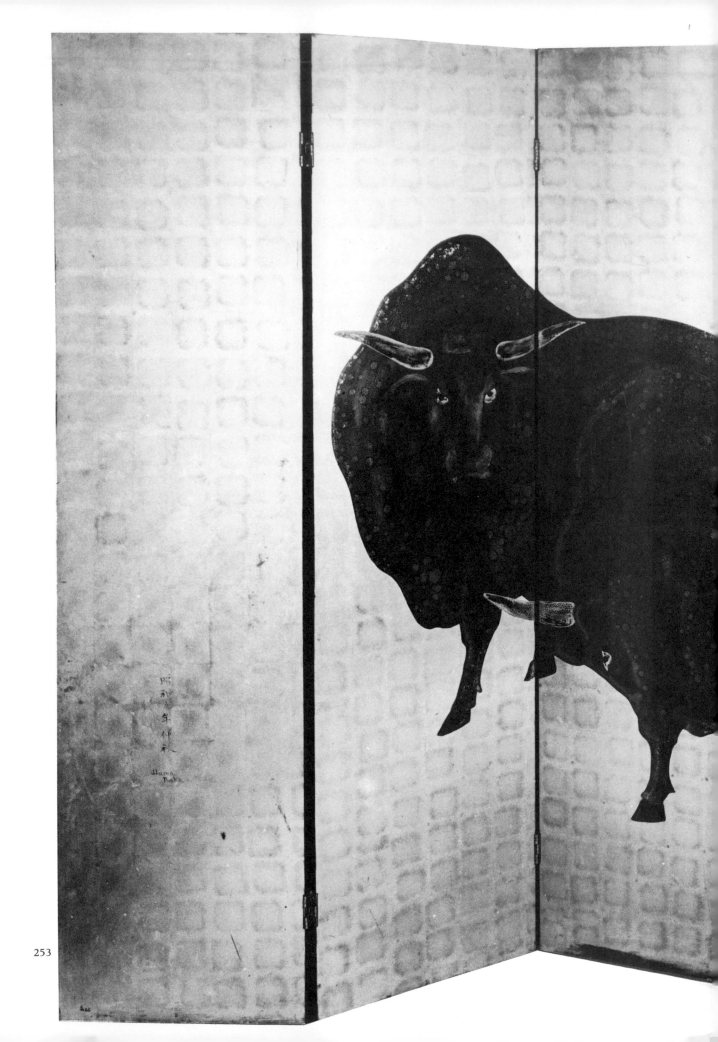

253

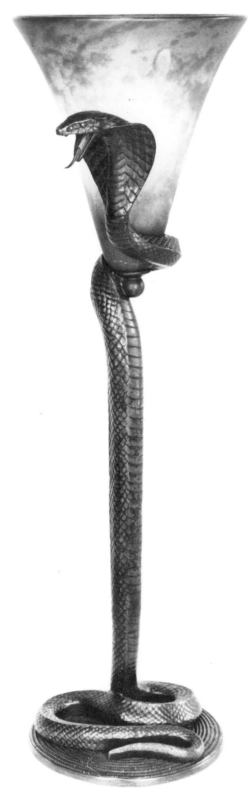

254. EDGAR BRANDT, Lamp, *Bronze and alabaster.*
Brandt was the leading ironsmith of the 1920s. Sometimes the alabaster shade in this model is replaced by a glass one made by Daum.

8   METALWORK

A wide variety of metalwork was made in the Art Deco period, and it is more convenient to deal with this production in several sections or groups, beginning with work in forged iron, in bronze, and in that typically "modern" material, aluminum.

One of the first designers to envisage new possibilities for the use of forged iron in the home was Emile Robert, though his balustrades and doors have interlaced scrolls and flowers which make them reminiscent of Art Nouveau. In Robert's footsteps followed a number of other designers: the Nics brothers, Raymond Subès, Edouard Schenk, Richard Desvallières, A-G Szabo, Paul Kiss and (the best-known of them) Edgar-William Brandt. The repertoire was extremely characteristic—it included waterfalls, leaves, leaping deer, volutes, stylized flowers and abstract "Cubist" motifs. Ironwork in this style was used for elevator doors, radiator covers and swing doors between rooms, as well as for garden gates, balconies and shopfronts.

Iron was frequently used architecturally, in conjunction with glass, for ceilings and walls. This was in no sense an innovation—it had been used thus, and on the largest scale, at the Crystal Palace in London (1851) and the Grand Palais in Paris (1900).

René Lalique designed massive glass doors in metal frames for his own house on the Cours Albert 1er, for Jacques Doucet, and for the French consulate in Brussels—this last commission was undertaken in conjunction with Emile Robert.

A fashionable use of iron was to employ it to make the bases of consoles and of pedestal tables—these usually had tops in either marble or glass—and the details of the ironwork base would be repeated in the chandeliers and wall appliqués to be found in the same room. Design of this type were created by Sue et Mare, Raymond Subès, Fernand Nathan, Louis Marjorelle, Maurice Dufrêne, Edouard Schenk and of course by Brandt himself.

Brandt also collaborated with Daum to make superb standard lamps in the form of a rearing serpent, holding the shade in the one of the coils of his textured and patinated body. Paul Kiss, a remarkable technician who collaborated with Brandt and who has since been somewhat overshadowed by him executed and signed a few lamps of this type.

Most Art Deco lights were, however, rather traditional in form—they might be decorated with stylized floral ornament, or with waterfalls of crystal or glass drops. But certain steps forward were nevertheless taken, in solving the decorative problems posed by electricity. One point was that visible lamps now did not need to be so bright, since concealed and diffused ceiling lights were frequently used.

Pierre Chareau, the architect, and Jean Perzel, devised lighting fixtures made of overlapping planes of glass which still seem astonishingly modern. Perzel received many commissions from abroad for his chromed metal standard lamps, and wall appliqués made of opaque white and matte glass. His clients included Henry Ford of Detroit, the Maharajah of Indore (whose entire palace was furnished with Art Deco), the Emperor of Annam and the King of Siam. J. Le Chevalier, with the assistance of R. Koechlin, made table-lamps that were like pieces of machinery, brute metal slabs with the screws visible, while Le Corbusier invented a desk-lamp of angle-poise type (his innovations were more acceptable in a field of design which had little tradition of its own). Jean Goulden, the silversmith and enameller, preferred, on the other hand, to disguise the utilitarian aspect of lighting appliances, and created a night light, now in an American collection, which looks like a Cubist sculpture.

One extremely individual designer who concerned himself with lighting was Albert-Armand Rateau. His standard lamps, seats and tables in bronze are unlike anything else produced in the twenties. He began his career by executing interiors for the decorator, ceramist and collector Georges Hoentschel, and then worked for the Maison Alavoine between 1905 and 1914. After the war he created furniture and furnishings for a prestigious clientele. It included Jeanne Lanvin, George Blumenthal, the Baroness Eugène de Rothschild and the Duchess of Alba.

Rateau's manner was instantly recognizable. Against lacquered and painted walls he would place seats formed like scallop shells, with legs made of horns or deer. These seats are reminiscent of Chippendale grotto chairs. The alabaster shades of the lamps were supported by swan's necks or writhing serpents. With the help of his collaborator, Paul Plumet, Rateau conjured up the atmosphere of the ancient Mediterranean, so it seemed as if some rich archaeological site had been brought back to life, the dark patinated bronze contrasting with the yellow, blue and silver of the upholstery and the walls.

Turning towards the future, rather than evoking the past, many designers broke entirely with tradition by using aluminum and chromed metal in conjunction with leather and glass. When it was first shown in the mid-twenties, furniture of this type was received with cries of indignation. People said it was disagreeable to touch, and fit only for a dentist's surgery. The pioneering designers—René Herbst, J. Adnet, Charlotte Perriand, Le Corbusier, Jeanneret, Mallet-Stevens—maintained their enthusiasm, because they felt that this was the furniture that reflected their own social ideals, the furniture of the future. Some industrialists agreed with them—Marcel Breuer, the great Bauhaus designer, was given a commission by Thonet, the firm who, in the mid nineteenth century, had made their name and their fortune with the new industrially produced bentwood furniture. But the furniture designed by "modernists," such as those whom we have just listed, is not and never was true Art Deco. Men such as Le Corbusier recognized that the luxurious handmade furniture produced by a man like Ruhlmann was the antithesis of everything which they themselves stood for.

Work in copper and pewter forms a second group under our chosen heading of "metalwork." It was Art Nouveau which had brought these materials to prominence, and with Art Deco their importance receded a little, though beautiful objects continued to be made by a few craftsmen. Jean Dunand is again the leading name in this field, as he is in the field of lacquer. What Dunand produced lacks the aggressively hand-made look characteristic of the objects made by members of the Arts and Crafts Movement in England, but was, nevertheless, the product of an arduous process of hand labor.

A bowl or vase would begin as a piece of copper sheet. This would be placed on a wooden trestle and hit with a wooden hammer, so that gradually the metal curved. At the end of each series of beatings, the metal was placed in a kiln—this took place perhaps twenty or thirty times—was heated, and then cooled again before work began once more. At last the vase or bowl was formed, and was ready for the next process. A long steel instrument was tapped into the metal from the inside, so that the decoration appeared in relief. In pieces of the highest quality, fillets of precious metal, silver or gold, would be hammered into grooves gouged in the surface, and then beaten until perfectly flat and smooth.

Dunand at first made fruit and gourd forms, but his shapes grew plainer and more classical with time; they were often ornamented with designs in lacquer which had, according to a contemporary critic, "a primitive greatness."

Other metalworkers also chose to work in copper. One was Dunand's pupil, Claude Linossier, who deliberately refused to disguise or patinate the reddish color of the copper, so that the metal retained a crude, rough look. Other coppersmiths were Luclanel, who worked for Christofle, Berthe Cazin, Gaston Bigard, Edouard Schenk and Jean Serrière.

Pewter was used by Jean Després, Tetard Frères and Maurice Daurat, chiefly for vases and for tea and coffee services—the latter had heavy bodies and handles in teak or ebony. The silver made during the twenties varies widely in quality. Ordinary table services were made mechanically. A steel matrix was made from a plaster mould, and the design was then stamped with a power-press into the metal sheet. Top-class pieces were made by hand. Paul Follot for Laparra and Sue et Mare designed services which were transitional in style between the ornateness of Art Nouveau and the starkness of Art Deco.

The most radical changes were made within the framework provided by firms which were already well-known and long-established, though there were also a few independent craftsmen such as Georges Després and Gerard Sandoz. Some companies, such as the Maison Boin-Taburet, clung to tradition, and altered their products only slightly to accommodate changing taste, but others—among them the Maison Laparra, Puiforcat, Cardeilhac, Tetard Frères and Christofle—made silver between 1925 and 1937 which is impeccably simple and functional. Despite the use of ivory and hardwood for handles, of lapis, aventurine, jade and occasionally rock-crystal for knobs, a teapot by one of these firms remained a teapot, and was not disguised under bouquets of flowers and bunches of fruit as such objects had been at the turn of the century. The two great names in Art Deco silver are Jean Tetard and Jean Puiforcat. The work of each has a logical harmony, and displays the naked beauty of the metal.

With the coming of the Depression, many firms were forced to move away from their traditional homes in in the large houses of the Marais district, and settle in the eighth *arrondisement*, but most recovered enough to show excellent work in the 1937 exhibition.

Enamels, popular with Art Nouveau designers, enjoyed continuing popularity with their Art Deco successors, but were of course differently used. There was a distinct fashion for jewellery enamelled in bold colors—deep scarlets, blacks and blues. These colors appear on bracelets, geometrically patterned cigarette cases, cufflinks and watch-cases.

One craftsman who, unlike the majority of his contemporaries, carried out his own designs for silver and enamels himself, rather than leaving them to be executed by others, was Jean Goulden. He made chunky boxes and jewellery, enriched with thick cloisonné enamels in blue, turquoise and white. These were influenced by the Byzantine enamels Goulden had seen on Mount Athos. He made, in addition to the objects already mentioned, enamelled plaques for book-bindings by F-L Schmied. Schmied, Goulden, Jean Dunand and Paul Jouve were friends, and often exhibited their work together.

Another member of the group was the sculptor, Gustave Miklos. He also designed enamel plaques and jewellery, but the enamels are thinner and opaque. These enamels, which show either abstract designs or Miklos' characteristic elongated figures, are extremely rare.

Enamels of quite another kind were created by Camille Fauré. Fauré worked at the Limoges factory, and Limoges was a town which had for centuries been associated with the enameller's craft. Faure's translucid sugary pinks, blues and turquoises are found on metal vases of simple form—these had a great success at the 1925 exhibition.

255

255. CHRISTOLFE, Vases, *Oxidized copper inset with silvered metal.*

256. CAMILLE FAURÉ, Enamel vase. *The decoration is reminiscent of the Orphist paintings of Robert Delauney.*

256

257

257. ALBERT CHEURET, Clock.
*In the catalogue of the Minneapolis
Art Deco exhibition, Bevis Hillier
points out that this design resembles
ancient Egyptian hairstyles. The
Egyptian style was popular after
Howard Carter discoveries in 1922.*

258

259

260

258. JEAN DUNAND, Encrusted metal. *Dunand exhibited metalwork from 1905 onwards. His early vases have rough surfaces, like contemporary stoneware. He then began to use color, with brown or green patinas and metal encrustations. Later, he decorated his metal with lacquer.*

259. ARMAND RATEAU, Table, *Bronze and marble. Rateau created this model for Jean Lanvin, and a replica appeared in the bathroom decorated by Rateau for the Duchess of Alba in the Liria Palace, Madrid. This example belonged to the actress Jane Renouard who had a house entirely in Art Deco style at St. Cloud, built in 1924.*

260. JEAN DUNAND, Metal vases. *It is unusual to find floral ornamentation as in the central vase.*

261

261. JEAN DUNAND, Metal vases.
The right-hand piece, dated 1913, is in
black steel with 31 gold ornaments.

262. EDGAR BRANDT, Lamp, *Bronze*
and glass. Glass by Daum.

263. JEAN DUNAND, Metal vase.
Dunand's forms are usually classic and
depend on patination or relief detail
for their effect.

262

263

264

265

264. CLAUDIUS LIMOSSIER, Vase,
Encrusted copper and silver.

265. CLAUDIUS LIMOSSIER, Bowl,
Red copper encrusted with silver.

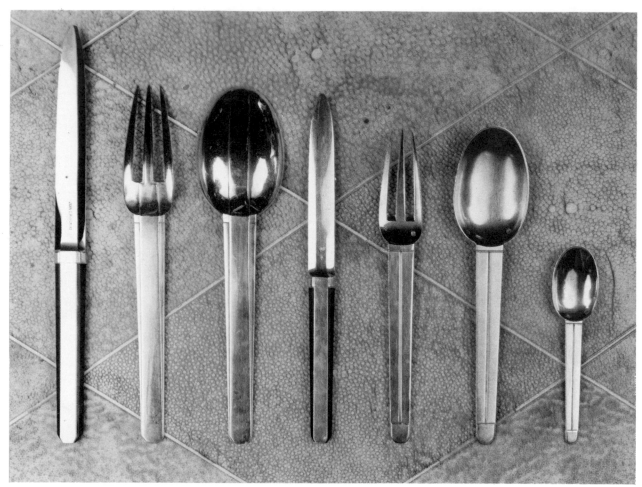

266

267

266. JEAN PUIFORCAT, Silver. *Puiforcat designed for the family firm in the 1920's. This table service, while modern and elegant, is at the same time serviceable.*

267. JEAN PUIFORCAT, Silver teaset, *Puiforcat showed the ability to design for traditional purposes while breaking away from past styles.*

268. JEAN PUIFORCAT, Covered tureen, *Silver.*

269

270

269. JEAN PERZEL, Wall light, *Chrome.*
Perzel was a specialist in lighting—
he worked for Henry Ford, the
Maharajah of Indore, the Emperor of
Imam and the King of Siam, as well
as making designs for the Normandie.

270. PAUL IRIBE, Candelabras, *Solid*
silver and rock crystal.
Iribe had a varied career—as a fashion
illustrator, interior decorator and
man-of-the-cinema-and-theater. He left
France for the United States in 1914
and did not return until 1929. On his
return he designed jewellery for Chanel.

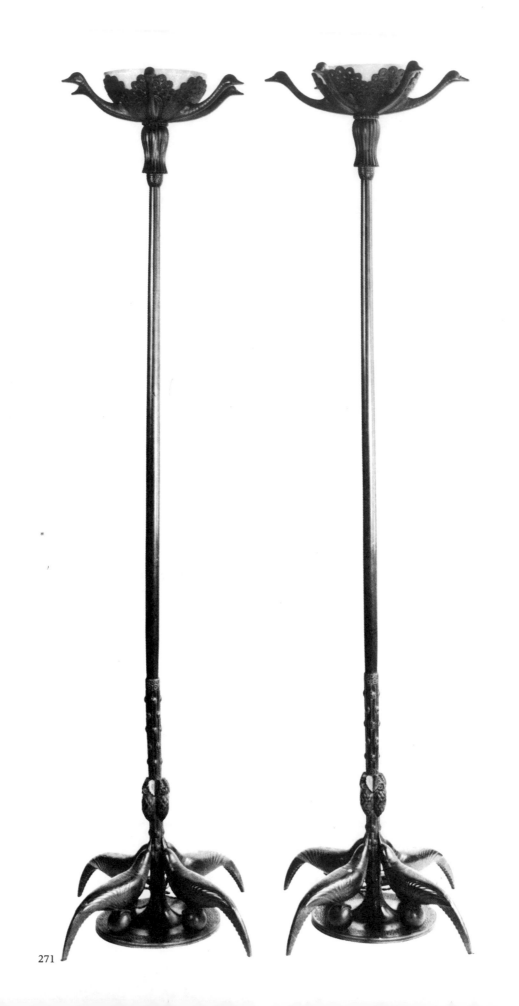

271

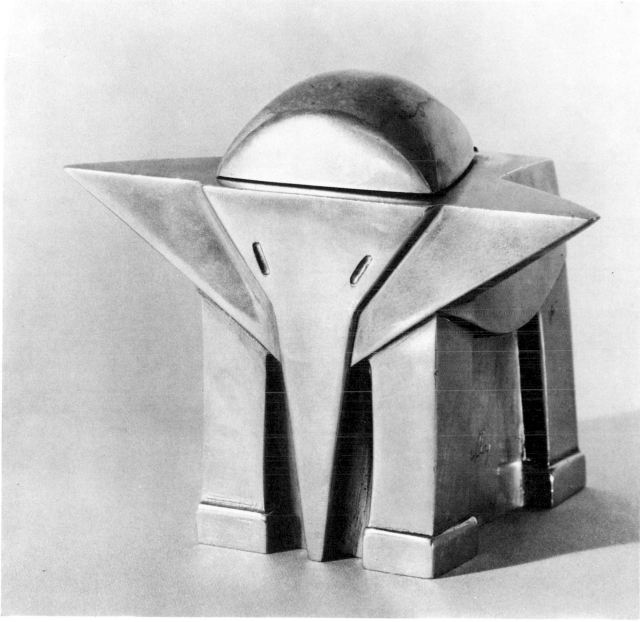

272

271. Armand Rateau, Pair of
standing lamps.
*Lamps of this type were made for
Jean Lanvin. Rateau's bronze
furniture in neo-classical style was
displayed against a background of
cornflower blue—"bleu Lanvin" and
sienna yellow.*

272. Yelly, Inkwell, *Silvered bronze.*

273. GEORGES FOUQUET, Pendant, *lacquer jet and onyx; or in the*
Frosted rock crystal, platinum and *preferred colors of the time with topaz,*
brilliants. *jade, malachite, coral, lapis, emeralds*
Fashionable jewels were either black *and rubies in addition to gold and*
and white; crystal, platinum, white *enamels.*
gold and silver, diamonds, black

9 JEWELLERY

The great Art Nouveau jewellers created masterpieces of miniature sculpture, with finely chased naturalistic leaves and flowers, fantastic heads and writhing serpents. Their materials were gold, enamels and baroque pearls, which suggested a rivalry with Renaissance goldsmiths. At its most extreme, this symbolist Art Nouveau jewellery was not intended to be worn. The jewels were collector's objects. Meanwhile, prosperous members of the bourgeoisie continued to wear jewels of traditional style—heavy bracelets, necklaces and tiaras set with diamonds, sapphires, rubies and emeralds—or garnets, if the worst came to the worst. The purpose of these flamboyant adornments was to be the visible sign of prosperity.

During the twenties, a similar division between "art" jewellery and "money" jewellery continued to exist, though the opposition between the two extremes was perhaps less marked. The established jewellers of the Place Vendôme and the rue de la Paix—Cartier, Van Cleef et Arpels, Chaumier, Mauboussin, Boucheron—adapted their work to the current taste for greater simplicity, sometimes re-setting a customer's stones if the mounts had come to seem too old-fashioned. Some pieces went out of favor. Short hair killed the hair comb and the big hatpin. Rings were now made of one large stone, ideally a fine diamond from the mines in the Transvaal, Brazil or India. A Dutch diamond-cutting firm set up at Versailles and introduced several new ways of faceting, including the baguette cut. Pearls were much in demand, as they were part of every fashionable woman's uniform. The rich wore real ones from the Persian gulf, but tinted fake ones—pink, grey and blue—were acceptable.

Other highly fashionable items, in addition

to a string of pearls, were little watches with diamond bracelets, and long drop earrings. The latter often had a spherical stone at the tip.

The work of certain "name" designers had more individuality than this. Some, such as Henri Vever, George Fouquet and René Lalique, were the survivors of the Art Nouveau period. What they made in the twenties was less extravagant than their earlier work. Lalique, who had used colored glass pastes in gold settings to great effect during the 1890's, now made pendants in transparent colored glass decorated with nymphs, animals or leaves. These were hung on the end of long silk cords.

Some jewellery, mostly not the most valuable kind, abandoned restraint and became as consciously fashionable, and therefore almost as ephemeral, as clothes, In 1911, Paul Iribe created tie pins and diadems in brilliants and colored pearls, and also brooches and aigrettes to fix on the newly fashionable turbans, in response to the current vogue for oriental dress. Another fashion illustrator, George Barbier, designed a collection for Cartier in 1919.

The couturière Coco Chanel carried this development to its logical conclusion by being the first to introduce costume jewellery—frankly fake stuff designed to be be worn as long as it was fashionable and then discarded. Patou presented jewellery with his dress collection in 1927, and Schiaparelli was later to design surrealist brooches as well as surrealist hats.

Despite the innate conservatism of retailers and customers, both the twenties and thirties managed to establish distinctive styles. Many early Art Deco jewels, for example, made use of cloisonné enamels, with particular emphasis on the metal mounts in gold, silver and platinum. Curved rather than geometric and generally small in size, jewels such as these were signed by Charles Rivaud and his son André Rivaud, Henry Miault, René Robert, Gerald Sandoz and Paul Brandt. Jewels were made by leading metalworkers—Jean Serrière, the Nics brothers, and Edgar Brandt.

Later, striking jewels were designed by the future members of the *Union des Artistes Modernes,* who, it will be remembered, wanted to break with past styles and to design something truly modern, Their work was architecturally conceived, balancing one plane against another, a rectangle against a curve. Jewellery now fell into two categories: the black-and-white and the colored. Jewels of the first kind were made of platinum, white gold, silver, pavé-set diamonds, rock-crystal, black lacquer and black onyx. The alternative was to use gold, enamel, topaz, malachite, jasper, coral, emeralds, rubies and turquoise matrix. The strength of platinum allowed open-claw settings rather than the traditional metal cup, and this gave new brilliancy to transparent stones. Georges and Jean Fouquet, Gerard Sandoz, Raymond Templier and Jean Desprès were leading practitioners of the developed Art Deco style, and their work was to be seen at the 1925 and 1937 exhibitions.

During the thirties, new fashions came in. Heavy bracelets, sometimes combined with a second thin one, were worn on each wrist. Double clips, worn either as a brooch on the shoulder or in the hat, or else caught in the neckline of a dress, were almost obligatory, as pearls had been during the twenties. For these items, pavé-set diamonds were generally used, often in "Moorish" or "Egyptian" style, but rhinestones and other imitations, together with the industrialization of the craft, enabled more people to wear jewellery than ever before.

No account of the epoch would be complete without a brief description of some of the characteristic *bibelots* of the time. They convey its flavor even more accurately than the designs used for jewellery. In the 1912–20 period, Clément Mère made boxes, buttons, umbrella handles, bracelets, pendants and fans in ivory, shagreen gold and semi-precious stones. The delicately worked surfaces were carved with insects, petals, shells or seaweed—the prevailing tones were white, topaz and bronze. Henri Hamm and Georges Bastard worked in wood, tortoise shell, horn, ivory and mother-o'-pearl. Bastard was particularly well-known for his fans. Madame O'Kin, the wife of the ceramist Henri Simmen, made jewellery, paper-knives and other objects in ivory and hardstone.

The colonial exhibitions staged at Marseilles in 1922 and at Vincennes in 1931 helped to sustain the fashion for ivory and ebony. So did the craze for primitive, particularly African, art. Nancy Cunard, at one and the same time a famous beauty of the period, and a well-known intellectual, made a trade-mark of the African ivory bracelets which covered her slender arms from wrist to elbow.

During the twenties, accessories such as powder compacts, watch and cigarette cases, buttons, cuff-links etc. were made in richly colored enamels and in lacquer. Patterns were generally geometric, but there was also a fashion for Chinese themes, partly suggested by the feeling for Chinese ceramics and other objects, and partly by the contemporary taste for lacquer, jade and coral, all of them "oriental" materials. Cartier and Lacloche, in particular, made a speciality of accessories with Chinese designs.

Compacts and cigarette cases became an indispensible accessory of the fashionable woman. The way in which she manipulated them established the view she had of herself—she used them as an eighteenth century dandy used his snuff-box. Sometimes the compact grew a little larger, and was turned into the "nécessaire" or "minaudière" which contained a lipstick, a compartment for powder, and also a mirror—it came in many different shapes, and could be flat and rectangular, octagonal, or take the form of a flattened cylinder. On occasion the lipstick was contained in a separate baton, which hung from a chain. A woman who made use of these fashionable toys was consciously or unconsciously trying to emphasize the degree to which she had identified herself with the new liberty of the post-war epoch—before this, women of breeding had neither smoked nor repaired their make-up in public. This is one reason why the shapes and ornamentation often provide extreme examples of the development of Art Deco style.

274. GEORGES LEPAPE, *Gouache. Dated 1927.*
Patou was the first couturier to present jewels with his dress collections in 1927. During the late twenties and early thirties, heavy bracelets were worn on each wrist, sometimes over the gloves, or as here singly with a narrow bracelet above.

275. (OVERLEAF)
GEORGES FOUQUET, *Necklace, Frosted rock crystal, platinum brilliants and topaz.*
Firms such as Cartier, Van Cleef and Arpels, Maboussin, Boucheron continue to make jewellery with colored stones for traditional clientele. Other designers such as Templier, George, and Jean Fouquet, Sandoz, Desprès and Paul Brandt, created jewels whose interest lies in the design rather than the intrinsic value of the stones.

276 (OVERLEAF)
JEAN FOUQUET *Pendant Platinum, coral, jet and brilliants*
Jean Fouquet, son of Georges, was also a member of the Union des Artistes Moderne. Jewels designed by this group were in harmony with short hair, simple straight clothes and an active life. Exhibited in Minneapolis Art Deco Exhibition.

277

277. RANSON, *Gouache.*
*Clips were the most popular pieces of
jewellery during the 1930's. They were
made in all materials from diamonds
to paste and plastic, and could often be
joined together to make a brooch.
They were worn at the neck of the
dress, or could be clipped to a hat as
in this illustration.*

278. RAYMOND TEMPLIER, Bracelet,
*Platinum, white gold, onyx and
diamonds. Exhibited in Amersfoot,
Holland, 1972.*
*Templier was a member of the Union
des Artistes Moderne formed in 1930.
He made strong, heavy jewellery with
panels of brilliants which set off the
broad band of metal.*

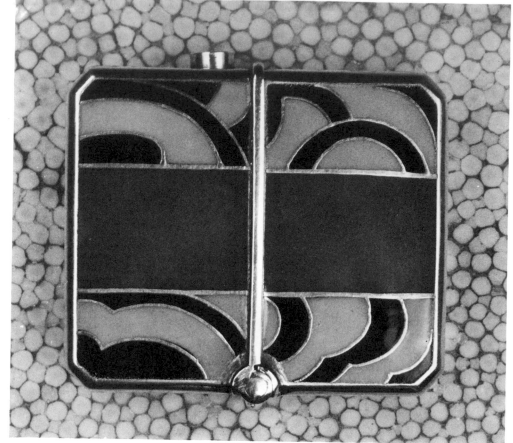

279

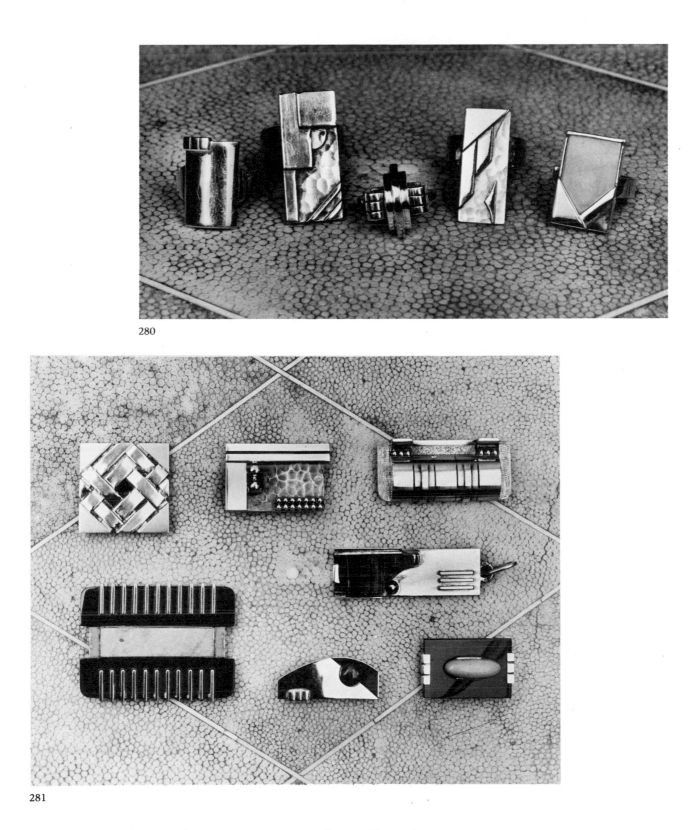

280

281

279. ANON. Watch, *Enamel.*

280. JEAN DESPRÈS, Rings.
Big rings were fashionable, often set with a single block of hardstone.

281. JEAN DESPRÈS, Jewellery, *Silver.*
Desprès showed his work at the Paris salons and at the exhibitions of 1925 and 1937. He incorporated small glass panels painted by Etienne Cournault.

283

282. RAYMOND TEMPLIER, Handbag, *Silver and velvet.*

283. TANUSIER, Compact, *Silvered metal lacquer with eggshell and carved hardstone.*
Chinese motifs are often found in the jewellery and on the cigarette cases, compacts, etc. designed in the 1920s.

284. RAYMOND TEMPLIER, Rings and bracelet, *Silver;* Brooch, *Silver and lapis lazuli.*
Made for the artist's wife. Exhibited in Minneapolis Art Deco Exhibition and Amersfoot, Holland, 1972.

285. (OVERLEAF)
GEORGES FOUQUET, Necklace, *Frosted rock crystal platinum, turquoise matrix, jet and baroque pearls.*

284

BIBLIOGRAPHY

GENERAL EXHIBITION CATALOGUES

1966. *Les Années 25*. Musée des Arts Décoratifs, Paris. Catalogue by Yvonne Brunhammer. Two volumes: 1) Art Deco, Bauhaus, l'Esprit Nouveau; 2) collection of the museum. Biographies.

1971. *Art Deco*. Minneapolis Institute of Arts, Minneapolis, USA catalogue by Bevis Hillier. Good bibliography by Robert K. Brown. Kitsch, revivals and pastiches as well as top art deco.

1971. *Art Deco*. Finch College Museum of Art, New York, Catalogue by Judith Applegate. French and American applied arts.

1973. *Die Zwangwiger Jahre. Kontraste eines Jahrzehnts*. Kunstgewerbemuseum, Switzerland. Catalogue by Erika Billiter. Architecture, photography, film stills and theatre as well as decorative arts. Bauhaus, De Stijl, Constructivism and Art Deco.

1974. *Objekte der Zwanziger Jahre*. Stuck Villa, Munich, Germany. Catalogue by Gabriele Sterner. French art deco, some Bauhaus and Vienna Succession. Biographies of artists.

GENERAL BOOKS

Battersby, Martin. *The Decorative Twenties*. Studio Vista, London, 1969. Review of French, American and English art deco designers. Short bibliography. Concentrates on the social-fashion side.

Battersby, Martin. *The Decorative Thirties*. Studio Vista, London, 1971. French, American and English interior decoration. Short bibliography.

Brunhammer, Yvonne. *Lo Style 1925*. Fratelli Fabbri, Milan, 1966. Based on the collection in the reserves of the Musée des Arts Décoratifs, Paris.

Frank, Nona. *Les Années 30*. Pierre Horay, Paris, 1969. Social history, politics, films, Surrealism, some decorative arts.

Herbst, René. *25 Années: Union des Arts Modernes*. Salon des Arts Ménagers, Paris, 1955. Work of the architectural school.

Hillier, Bevis. *Art Deco*. Studio Vista, London, 1968. European and American Art Deco, emphasising the popular, and the kitsch. One of the first modern books about the style.

Mourey, Gabriel. *Histoire Générale de l'Art Français de la Revolution à Nos Jours: l'Art Décoratifs*. Librarie de France, 1925. Good general appreciation of the Art Deco style.

Quénioux, Gaston. *Les Arts Décoratifs Modernes*. Librarie Larousse, Paris, 1925. Many photographs, one of the best books of its kind, divided into sections; architecture, furniture, glass, ceramics, etc.

Veronesi, Giula. *Into the Twenties. Style and Design 1909–1929*. Italian edition Vallecci, Florence, 1966. English edition Thames and Hudson, 1968. Life and times in Europe. Less strong on the decorative arts. Biographies of the main figures of the period.

Verne and Chavance. *Pour Comprendre l'Art Décoratif Moderne en France*. Hachette, Paris, 1925. A pocket book with everything from aeroplanes and trains to fashion and decoration. Good general idea of the style, although few details.

PAINTING, ILLUSTRATIONS, BOOKS, POSTERS

Crespelle, Jean-Paul. *La Folle Epoque. Des Ballets Russes au Surréalisme*. Hachette, Paris, 1968. Cocteau, the artists of Montparnasse and the follies and fantasies of the twenties.

Deville, Etienne. *La Reliure Française*. G. van Oest, Paris et Bruxelles, 1931. A section on Art Deco binding.

Hillier, Bevis. *Posters*. Weidenfeld and Nicolson, London, 1969. Concentrates mainly on the 1890's but one of the few books to give an idea of Art Deco posters.

Galerie de Luxembourg. *Illustrateurs des Modes et Manières en 1925*. Exhibition catalogue, Paris, 1973. Fashion and book illustrators, detailed list of each artist's published work.

SCULPTURE

Basler, Adolphe. *La Sculpture Moderne en France*. G. Crès, & Cie. Paris, 1928. Decorative sculptors as well as the major ones.

Moussinac. *Le Meuble Français Moderne*. Hachette, Paris, 1925. A choice of the leading designers. Few illustrations.

Olmer, Pierre. *Le Mobilier Français d'Aujourd'hui*. G. van Oest, Paris et Bruxelles, 1925. Like all the books in this series, invaluable information and biographies of the artists.

FASHION

Poiret, Paul. *En habillant l'époque*. Grasset, Paris, 1930. Poiret's account of his rise and fall in the world of fashion and interior decoration.

Rochas, Marcel. *Vingt-Cinq Ans d'Elegance à Paris*. Pierre Tisné, Paris, 1951. A photographic account of all that was most elegant in the fashionable circles, the theater, the arts, from 1925–1950.

White, Palmer. *Poiret*. Studio Vista, London, 1973. A good account of Poiret's influence and the artists who worked for him.

CERAMICS

Heuser, Hans-Jorgen. *Franzoscher Keramik 1830–1910*. Exhibition Catalogue, Cologne, Hanover and Darmstadt, 1974–1975. Good choice of the best of French ceramics.

Sèvres, *L'Art de la Poterie en France de Rodin à Dufy*. Exhibition Musée National de Porcelaine de Sèvres, 1971. Catalogue, special number of *Cahiers de la Céramique*. First important exhibition of its kind of French Art Nouveau and Art Deco ceramics. Biographical notices and short bibliography.

Valotaire, Marcel. *La Céramique Française Moderne*. G. van Oest, Paris et Bruxelles, 1930. The best survey yet of Art Nouveau/Art Deco ceramics.

GLASS

Polak, Ada. *Modern Glass*. Faber and Faber, London, 1962. The best book on 20th century glass.

Rosenthal, Léon. *La Verrerie Française depuis cinquante ans*. G. van Oest, Paris et Bruxelles, 1927. A good early book on Art Nouveau and Art Deco glass.

LACQUER

Galerie de Luxembourg. *Jean Dunand, Jean Goulden*. Exhibition catalogue, Paris, 1973. Foreword, Yvonne Brunhammer. Excellent survey of Dunand's work and the technique of lacquering.

Lorac-Gerbaud, Andrée. *L'Art du Laque*. Dessain et Tolra, Paris, 1974. Concentrates on Oriental lacquer but gives biographical details of the most important lacquerers of the 1920's.

METALWORK

Bouilhet, Tony. *L'Orfèverie Française au XX Siècle*. Emile-Paul Frères, Paris, 1941. Elegant book showing the change from Art Nouveau to Art Deco silver.

Hughes, Graham. *Modern silver throughout the world, 1880–1967*. Studio Vista, London, 1967. Well documented. Biographies.

JEWELLERY

Hughes, Graham. *Modern Jewellery*. Studio Vista, London, 1963. Photographic account of 20th century jewellery. Biographies and short bibliography.